ENHANCING LEADERSHIP IN COLLEGES AND UNIVERSITIES

ENHANCING LEADERSHIP IN COLLEGES AND UNIVERSITIES

A Case Approach

By

ARTHUR SANDEEN

University of Florida
Gainesville, Florida

CHARLES C THOMAS • PUBLISHER, LTD.
Springfield • Illinois • U.S.A.

Published and Distributed Throughout the World by

CHARLES C THOMAS • PUBLISHER, LTD.
2600 South First Street
Springfield, Illinois 62704

©2011 by CHARLES C THOMAS • PUBLISHER, LTD.

ISBN 978-0-398-08600-8 (Hard)
ISBN 978-0-398-08601-5 (Paper)
ISBN 978-0-398-08602-2 (ebook)

Library of Congress Catalog Card Number: 2010029351

With THOMAS BOOKS *careful attention is given to all details of manufacturing
and design. It is the Publisher's desire to present books that are satisfactory as to their
physical qualities and artistic possibilities and appropriate for their particular use.*
THOMAS BOOKS *will be true to those laws of quality that assure a good name
and good will.*

Printed in the United States of America
CR-R-3

Library of Congress Cataloging-in-Publication Data

Sandeen, Arthur, 1938–
　Enhancing leadership in colleges and universities : a case approach / by
Arthur Sandeen
　　p.　cm.
　ISBN 978-0-398-08600-8 (hard) -- ISBN 978-0-398-08601-5 (pbk.)
　1. Universities and colleges--Administration--Case studies. 2. Case
method. 3. Universities and colleges--United States--Business management.
4. Educational leadership--Case studies. I. Title.

　LB2341.S245 2010
　378.1'010973--dc22

　　　　　　　　　　　　　　　　　　　　　　　　　　2010029351

PREFACE

College and university administrators in 2011 face academic, financial, political, and personnel issues that make their jobs very challenging. The various constituents with whom they work frequently represent competing and contradictory agendas, placing these leaders in situations where they cannot possibly please everyone. Yet, despite these problems, talented and dedicated men and women continue to be attracted to administrative positions in colleges and universities.

Since the economic recession of 2008, the challenges facing college and university leaders have become even more daunting. In public and private institutions, budget shortfalls and declining endowments have forced academic administrators to make difficult decisions about the curriculum, facilities, departmental structures and organization, and, of course, faculty and staff. State legislatures, faculty, accrediting associations, parents, and alumni are also increasingly scrutinizing the decisions made by college and university leaders and holding them accountable for their actions. Governing boards of both public and private institutions are paying closer attention to the day-by-day operations of their campuses and, in particular, raising the performance expectations of their presidents.

In addition to the economic problems facing higher education leaders in 2011, the tragic shooting incidents at Virginia Tech University, Northern Illinois University, and other institutions have focused more public attention on the actions of campus officials. These events have increased the expectations for institutions to provide support services to students, faculty, and staff that could have scarcely been imagined only 10 years ago.

In view of the serious challenges facing college and university administrators, it is encouraging to note the increased interest in improving leadership knowledge and skills. Professional associations representing presidents, provosts, academic deans, and fundraising, student affairs, and administrative affairs officers all sponsor leadership seminars and conferences for their members. Moreover, the amount and quality of applied research on decision making, organizational cultures, assessment, and management have increased. Many senior officers in college and universities participate in intensive, interactive leadership institutes designed to help them enhance their skills. Several informal associations of presidents, provosts, and other senior leaders exist, where groups of 15 to 20 administrators from similar institutions meet periodically to share mutual concerns and to explore solutions to their problems. It is also increasingly recognized that serving in a major leadership role in a college or university can be a very stressful experience, and more attention is being given to healthful strategies to support and retain successful administrators.

There is no evidence that there is only one approach to achieving success in college and university leadership. For some, reading in the vast literature on leadership is useful; for others, attending seminars or actually enrolling in a graduate academic program is preferable. Many leaders seek out their colleagues for advice and insights, while others find seminars and conferences more useful. Some leaders depend on long-time mentors to provide support and honest feedback about their work.

This book presents an additional option to college and university administrators in their efforts to enhance their leadership skills. The case study approach to improving insights and skills in leadership is predicated on the belief that leadership is learned, that it is a complex process demanding excellent analytic and personal skills, and that it often requires courage to act and to live with the consequences of one's actions. The book includes 18 cases on a variety of issues being faced by college and university leaders. Its purpose is to encourage administrators to enhance their ability to make decisions by focusing on the decision-making process and by thinking about the consequences of the various options available to them. These cases can be most valuable when discussed and debated in small groups, but they can also be read and studied individually. The options presented in each case can be expanded by those studying and discussing them or revised to meet their personal preferences. Questions to encourage further discussion are presented at the end of each case, as well as a brief list of suggested readings related to the case. No single option is intended to be the "correct" one; the options are presented to illustrate some of the choices leaders have in addressing the issue in the case study and to suggest the possible consequences involved.

The cases are organized into four sections: (1) Raising Money and Funding of Services, (2) Athletics and Facilities, (3) Academic Policies and Issues, and (4) Student Services Issues. The cases represent realistic but fictitious issues at a variety of colleges and universities. Of course, the issues, the names of the institutions, and the names of the various administrators mentioned in the book are fictitious. Any resemblance to any actual institution or person is entirely coincidental.

A.S.

ACKNOWLEDGMENTS

Having spent more than 40 years as an administrator and faculty member at three land-grant universities, I have a long-time interest in leadership and exploring new ways of learning more about it. I have learned from reading and studying leadership theories, from personal accounts of successful leaders, and from my own experience in responding to issues and initiating new programs and policies.

I have learned the most about leadership from my interactions with outstanding and dedicated colleagues in my work at Iowa State Uni- versity, Michigan State University, and the University of Florida. I am grateful to my colleagues at these institutions for their insights and knowledge.

For many years, I have taught graduate students enrolled in educational leadership courses and seminars, and I continue to learn from these outstanding students. I have also enjoyed following their subsequent careers as leaders in many colleges and universities. This book is dedicated to these fine students, with sincere thanks for the privilege of being their teacher.

CONTENTS

ENHANCING LEADERSHIP IN COLLEGES AND UNIVERSITIES

Chapter 1

CASE STUDIES I: RAISING MONEY AND FUNDING SERVICES

CHANGING THE FUNDRAISING STRATEGY AT
  STANTOWNE UNIVERSITY

FUNDING PSYCHOLOGICAL SUPPORT SERVICES AT
  MASTERTOWN UNIVERSITY

RETHINKING BECKINGTOWN COLLEGE'S FINANCIAL
  AID POLICY

A FUNDRAISING DILEMMA AT PACKHURST COLLEGE

CHANGING THE FUNDRAISING STRATEGY AT STANTOWNE UNIVERSITY

SUMMARY OF THE CASE

Stantowne University is a large, private, research institution located in the Northeast. In 2010, its enrollment is 23,000 students, 5,000 of whom are in graduate and professional degree programs. The faculty are engaged in research and have been quite successful in attracting external funds for the past 20 years. While Stantowne has a good academic reputation, it has aspirations to become one of the nation's top research universities in the next 10 years. Its endowment is $750 million, and its newly appointed president knows he will have to increase this endowment significantly if Stantowne University is going to achieve its objective of moving up the academic ladder. During his hiring process, he examined the fundraising structure of the university and decided this would be one of the first major issues he would address. In his first 6 months as president, he discovered several problems and concerns regarding the fundraising organization and knew he needed to make some changes.

A DESCRIPTION OF STANTOWNE UNIVERSITY

Stantowne University was founded in 1835 by three Congregational ministers as a college to prepare young men for the clergy and for teaching. It is located in a city of 125,000. It grew slowly, and by 1910, it had increased its enrollment to 1,200 students mainly by expanding its curricular offerings. By 1950, the institution had become independent of any formal church affiliation, had grown to almost 8,000 students, and had developed graduate programs and new schools of architecture, engineering, and law. By 1975, its enrollment had grown to 20,000 students, and the university became increasingly visible and respected in its region. Stantowne's board of trustees decided to cap its enrollment at 23,000 in 1982, feeling this was a size that was most manageable and one that would allow the institution to meet its academic goals.

Stantowne University is reasonably competitive in its undergraduate admissions, but it does not attract as many student applicants with outstanding academic records as its three main competitor institutions in its region do. For many years, the university has been viewed as a relatively safe backup institution for fairly affluent students whose first choice was a more selective institution than Stantowne. Its cost of attendance is in the mid-range for private institutions, and students come from mostly throughout the Northeast and mid-Atlantic states.

The university is governed by a 45-member board of trustees appointed to 8-year terms by the board itself. This large board only meets once per year, but a 12-member executive board meets more often, and it is this group that effectively oversees the institution. About half of the board members are Stantowne University graduates, and the institution is fortunate that it is able to attract and retain outstanding professional, business, and civic leaders as members of its governing board. After Stantowne's president of the past 10 years retired in 2009, the board successfully completed a search for a new leader and was pleased to attract Anton Porter to become the new president. Porter had served as the provost of another private research university in the Midwest. He is a chemist and had worked in academic and administrative positions at three other institutions before his 5-year stint as a provost.

The fundraising efforts of the university are coordinated by the vice president for development and a full-time staff of some 40 professionals. The Stantowne University Foundation was established in 1965, considerably later than such organizations were in place at similar institutions. The Foundation has its own board, and the institution's president assumes a major leadership role in working with the Foundation board.

Stantowne University is especially proud of the growth of its graduate programs in recent years. Its faculty have been successful in attracting research funds from the National Science Foundation, various federal governmental agencies, and large corporations. Its graduate programs in electrical engineering, biological sciences, and chemistry are often listed among the top 50 in the country. The institution, led by its board of trustees, has high aspirations to achieve excellence in its academic programs, and it realizes that it has made good progress in the past 20 years but also knows it has a lot of work to do to meet its goals.

Stantowne University is well known in its region, and since the 1960s, its academic reputation has grown considerably. Its public visibility over the years has been enhanced by the success of its men's and women's intercollegiate athletic teams. Students, alumni, and other citizens of the state identify with these teams and love to attend various athletic events on the campus. The university has benefited from this attention and support over the years, as the athletic program has given the institution an effective platform to promote its academic programs.

The serious economic recession of 2008 presented Stantowne University with some difficult challenges. Its quite modest endowment has decreased in value by almost 20 percent, students and their families have pressed the institution for more financial assistance, and needed building repairs and new construction have been delayed or cancelled. About 35 staff positions have been eliminated, and faculty have not received a salary increase since 2008. The admissions office reports that applications for the entering freshman class are down by almost 10 percent, as more high school seniors are opting to apply to lower cost, public colleges and universities in the state and region.

THE STUDENTS AND THE FACULTY

The academic qualifications of the undergraduate students at Stantowne University have continued to improve during the past 20 years, and in 2010, almost all of them graduated in the top one third of their high school classes and in the top 25 percent of students taking the Scholastic Aptitude Test (SAT). They come to the institution from more than 30 states, although the great majority come from within the state and the immediate region. They come from fairly affluent families, and only about 8 percent of the undergraduates are minorities.

The university has made efforts over the past 10 years to increase the economic, racial, and ethnic diversity of the undergraduate student body, but it has not realized much success in this regard. The undergraduates like the institution once they are enrolled, and most stay until they graduate. The admissions office reports that the two main obstacles to attracting more first-generation, minority, and lower income students are Stantowne's high tuition and its comparatively low level of institution-based financial aid.

Because almost all of the university's students are enrolled on a full-time basis and almost half of them live on the campus, student life is active, with a strong emphasis on social and athletic-related activities. In recent years, undergraduates have become quite active in volunteer and community service programs, and increasing numbers of them have studied abroad for at least a semester, most frequently in Europe and Asia. There are several student residence halls on the campus. The institution is concerned that many of them are in need of repair and renovation, and some will have to be closed or torn down within the next few years unless something is done to improve their condition. Many of the undergraduates prefer to live in private apartments in the city, especially those who can afford to do so. Most of the residents of campus housing are freshmen.

The undergraduates at Stantowne University are increasingly borrowing money in order to continue their education at the institution. In 2010, over half of the students have taken out loans, and among this group, the average indebtedness at time of graduation is more than $50,000. This is a matter of concern to parents, the new president, and the board of trustees.

There is a student government association at the university, which oversees the 350 student organizations and allocates a modest student activity fee on their behalf. The student government association has focused almost all of its energy and attention on student-related issues for years and has not been active in politics or social-conscience matters.

The graduate students at the university are a much more diverse group than the undergraduates and come from institutions around the country and from 35 other countries. The graduate programs in engineering, biological sciences, and chemistry attract the best students and are the most competitive in terms of admissions.

Almost all of the doctoral students at Stantowne receive either a teaching and research assistantship or a fellowship during their graduate programs. However, in competing for graduate students, the university has not been as competitive as it would like to be due to budget constraints often related to its comparatively low endowment.

Because of graduate student unrest about their low stipends for their teaching and research assistantships and their frustration over not being eligible for university-supported health insurance, a new graduate student senate was formed in 2007, and it has petitioned the provost and graduate dean for more support each of the last 3 years. The graduate student senate has not had any success in these efforts and is increasingly impatient with the university administration for not being more responsive to its needs.

The faculty at Stantowne University has become more diverse and research oriented in the past 15 years. Almost one third of the faculty reached retirement age during this period, enabling the university to hire outstanding new faculty in almost every academic discipline. By almost any measure, the faculty is now stronger than it has ever been.

The faculty all teach undergraduates, but many find their most challenging work with graduate students and their own research. The university enjoyed great loyalty from its faculty for many years, and many of the faculty who retired in the past 15 years had taught at Stantowne for more than 30 years. The newest faculty enjoy their work at the university, but most of them are more committed to their own academic disciplines and research programs than they are to the institution, and the president, provost, and academic deans know that many of their most outstanding faculty are fairly easy targets in the competition for academic talent at other universities. Faculty salaries and benefits are fairly good but not at par with similar major private research universities. This has been a major issue for the past president and the board of trustees—perhaps the most important in its drive to improve the academic status of the university.

Most faculty are focused on activities in their own departments and colleges and until the past 2 or 3 years have not paid much attention to university-wide governance issues. The university senate is composed of faculty from all of the schools and colleges but had not been very active until the recession of 2008, when fears of cutbacks in academic programs, layoffs of staff, and static faculty salaries became serious concerns. As a result, the president and provost became much more visible with the university senate, defending their actions before the senate and sharing budgetary information with them.

THE ISSUE TO BE ADDRESSED IN THIS CASE STUDY

When Anton Porter assumed his new role as president of Stantowne University, he immediately began a careful assessment of the fundraising structure at the institution. In discussions with faculty and administrators, it became evident that the current vice president for development was not highly regarded by the deans of the colleges. Sandra Joyce has been in her role as vice president for development at Stantowne for 5 years, and previous to this position, she had served as the chief development officer at a medical school at a Midwestern university. There are 40 professional development officers at Stantowne, but most of them are responsible directly to the various college deans, who pay their salaries. One of the problems that president Porter quickly identified was lack of coordination among the various development officers and tension between them and Sandra Joyce. She is viewed by the deans as tentative in her decision-making style and not persuasive with the various constituents for the university. The president could see that this situation was not contributing positively toward an effective development program.

As President Porter continued his conversations with the college deans, it became obvious to him that, in their roles as fundraisers, the deans were not only competitive with one another, but they also "protected" potential donors from other colleges at Stantowne in their desire to secure large gifts from these donors for their own college. Worse still, the uncoordinated fundraising efforts of the college deans occasionally resulted in embarrassing situations with potential donors who had been approached by more than one college. This resulted in confusion and anger on the part of some potential donors, who justifiably wondered whether Stantowne University was paying adequate attention to its own organization.

President Porter knew it was important for him to get to know the members of the university's Foundation board, so he scheduled a number of luncheons with them in order to get to know how they view their role and to share his views about the university's future with them. He discovered, to his dismay, that most of the members of the Foundation board were not as sophisticated, influential, and dedicated as he had anticipated. Although the board has been helpful, its members are not as well connected to the professional and corporate communities as President Porter would like. Moreover, its members appar-

ently are not affluent and, during the past 10 years, have only contributed $1 million to the university.

When Anton Porter was discussing the president's position with the
Stantowne board of trustees during his candidacy, he asked the board
many searching questions about the development program, wonder-
ing why the institution's endowment was comparatively low. To his
surprise, the response from the board of trustees was that they thought
it was quite adequate and that they really had no important role in
helping the university in its private fundraising efforts. After a lengthy
discussion, Porter was able to convince the board that its support for
development efforts would be necessary if he were to become president of Stantowne University. After accepting the position as president, Porter again discussed the development program at the university with the board and was assured that he had its support in his effort
to enhance it.

As President Porter continued his assessment of the development
program at Stantowne, he confirmed that there has never been a university-wide fundraising campaign, focusing the university's effort on
a specific goal for a predetermined number of years. Porter understood that such an effort had not been made because previous presidents were not confident the institution could succeed in a campaign,
the current vice president for development does not appear to be a
strong leader, and the college deans essentially control their own
fundraising and do not want to weaken their own programs by shifting the emphasis to the university as a whole. Moreover, the Foundation board has not seen its own role as providing leadership to any
such effort.

President Porter also discussed the development program in detail
with the provost and the other vice presidents at Stantowne. In these
conversations, he found only mild support for the vice president for
development, Sandra Joyce as a leader, but sympathetic understanding for the dilemma they felt she faces—the college deans have the
power, and Joyce has no authority to direct their actions. They also
politely explained that the previous president spent little time on
fundraising and did not provide much direction to Vice President
Joyce. Finally, President Porter found that there was no institution-
wide mission statement or policy on fundraising and that Vice
President Joyce had essentially backed away from establishing one,
given the objections of the deans to any centralized fundraising strategy.

President Porter, after almost 6 months of careful listening, assessment, and thought, feels he knows the complex nature of the fundraising problems at his university. He also knows he must take the lead in ensuring that Stantowne University will significantly improve its fundraising program. The following are some options he may consider.

SOME OPTIONS FOR ADDRESSING THIS ISSUE

1. Invite a team of external consultants to the campus to advise President Porter what can be done to improve the fundraising program.

Although President Porter is confident of his own leadership ability and believes he understands the issues on his campus, he feels that an external team of recognized experts on university fundraising can raise awareness of the problems and lend credibility to his efforts to do something about them. The team would be composed of two experienced chief fundraising officers from other universities and one retired president from an institution that had a successful fundraising program. President Porter is confident that the consultants will say politely to Stantowne that its fundraising organization and strategy are not only unproductive and out of date, but also are not well directed to meet the institutions goals, especially of substantially increasing its endowment. President Porter must prepare the development vice president, her staff, and the college deans for the consultants' visit, informing them he is very serious about examining every aspect of Stantowne's development program. He knows bringing in the consultants will make them anxious and probably defensive about what they have been doing, but he wants to send a message early in his presidency that he is the leader, and he fully intends to make decisions to improve the university. He assures the Stantowne community beforehand that the consultants will be available to talk with anyone, and that their comments to the consultants will remain anonymous. However, the consultants' final report will be public. Finally, he announces that the university will give careful consideration to the consultant's, findings and recommendations but will make whatever decisions are necessary on its own.

In this option, the president is looking for an unbiased, external group to confirm what he already knows–that there are major problems in the fundraising structure and strategy at Stantowne and that significant changes are necessary if real improvements are to be achieved. He has to fight his own impatience, because he knows inviting the consultants to campus will delay what he thinks he could do faster, but he feels that this option will give him a better chance of achieving his goals. Moreover, he knows that in his first few months as Stantowne's new president, the way he approaches this major problem will help to define his decision-making style. He wants to involve others in debating and thinking about the issue, but he also wants his campus community to know that he is in charge and intends to do something positive about addressing important issues. As an experienced administrative leader, he knows there will be some cynicism, especially among the deans, about what they may feel is a plan on the president's part to invite consultants to the campus whose report will be used to justify what the president already intends to do. Finally, President Porter sees this exercise as a valuable opportunity to see whether Stantowne University can begin working and thinking as one institution, rather than a group of decentralized, almost autonomous colleges.

2. Appoint a campus-wide task force to study the problems and recommend an improved fund raising program at Stantowne University.

President Porter understands the long-established power of the college deans at Stantowne University. They have authority to establish the curriculum in their colleges, hire the faculty, and appoint their various department heads. In recent years, they have gained sufficient academic autonomy to control the general education program for their own students, virtually eliminating the former common campus- wide academic requirements for undergraduates. The college deans eagerly assumed responsibility for their own fundraising programs many years ago and work hard to protect their own interests. They have vigorously objected to any attempt by the previous president and the current vice president for development that they should share any of their private gifts with the institution-wide development office. Thus, in this option, President Porter feels a high-level task force, consisting of faculty, members of the Foundation board, prominent alumni, corporate leaders, college deans, and the provost, should be convened to study the fundraising program at Stantowne University and make recommendations to improve it. The president, in appointing the task force, clearly states his intention to find ways to increase the endowment and enable the university to become more competitive with other, similar institutions in its goal of achieving academic excellence.

In choosing this option, President Porter is buying some time but also acknowledging that he doesn't want to "take on" the college deans directly yet. He is reasonably confident that the broad-based task force he has appointed will not only reveal the limitations and problems of the fundraising program at Stantowne but also present some positive suggestions for improvement that can be implemented. He knows that the work of the task force will consume a good deal of time, but he thinks this is a necessary step in building awareness and support for needed changes. He knows he must be careful with those he asks to serve on the task force, because he does not want to be accused of appointing persons who are eager to support the new president. He also is aware that an institution-based task force may not be able or willing to confront the university's major shortcomings in its fundraising organization and strategy and, as a result, may not present him with a useful set of recommendations. If he does not like the task force's report, it may be difficult for him to do what he knows is needed.

3. Terminate the current vice president for development and hire a strong leader for this position at Stantowne University.

President Porter has high expectations for his university and knows that if success is going to be achieved, it will require outstanding and dedicated leaders in the major administrative positions. He was a successful dean and provost himself at other institutions, and he knows it requires hard work and a willingness to make tough decisions to accomplish positive academic results. After carefully assessing the performance of Sandra Joyce, the institution's vice president for development for the past 5 years and listening to other's views about her work, Porter decides to remove her from her position and hire a new leader for the fundraising operation. He is interested in the vice president for development at his previous university, because he was impressed with his leadership style; his ability to relate effectively to faculty, deans, donors, board members, and alumni; and his willingness to make tough decisions. Thus, in this option, President Porter decides new leadership is needed in the development office, and he moves ahead quickly and hires a person he is confident can move the institution toward its goals. He knows that the new person he has hired will have to win the confidence of the deans and many others at Stantowne, but he is confident that his new vice president will be able to do this. Porter also realizes that there are important organizational issues to address, but he feels that his new vice president will be able to overcome these especially because the deans and others clearly understand that the new vice president has the full backing of the president.

In this option, President Porter is placing his confidence in a person he views as a proven leader. With his own backing, the president intends to give the new development vice president the authority to build a strong fundraising program. The president expects a lot from the major members of his administrative team, and this is his first opportunity to demonstrate this fact. His will be a results-oriented presidency, and vice presidents in their various areas of responsibility will be expected to be strong and creative leaders. He will give them advice and support as needed, but he expects them to know what needs to be done and how to accomplish their goals. The new vice president, also an experienced administrative leader, knows there are significant risks for him in accepting this new position at Stantowne University. But he relishes the challenge and is thrilled at the opportunity to work for President Porter, a person he highly respects. He knows he is there to serve the president, and he will most likely only remain in the position so long as President Porter stays at Stantowne University. The president hired him because Porter has confidence in his ability to lead and accomplish his goals, and he does not want to let the president down.

4. Retain the current vice president for development, change the fundraising structure, and centralize the organization.

Anton Porter was hired as Stantowne's new president for his ability to lead and make decisions. He knows the board of trustees does not want to listen to excuses or endless reasons that little success is being realized in the fundraising

*program; it justifiably expects the president to address and resolve these prob-
lems! Thus, in this option, Porter is confident that he knows what the issues are
and he can greatly improve on the current situation by directing that some
changes will take place. He will retain the current vice president for development and significantly upgrade her authority by assuring the campus community (especially the college deans!) that she has full responsibility for the university's development program. The president will give her additional resources
to hire more staff, and will move the fundraisers now reporting to the college
deans to her staff. The college deans will now only pay a quarter of the development staff's salaries, and these staff will report to the vice president. Porter
will also direct the vice president for development to engage the faculty, deans,
alumni, Foundation board, and others in planning and implementing a 5-year
"Campaign for Stantowne" fundraising program. Finally, he makes it clear
that he will be actively engaged in fundraising efforts himself and expects a high
level of performance from all academic administrators at the university in helping to achieve the goals of the campaign.*

In this option, President Porter does not want to delay making needed decisions in the fundraising program, so he initiates the action he
feels is best. He knows his actions will anger and frustrate the college
deans and their supporters, but he is willing to look beyond their objections because he knows Stantowne must be moved to act as one institution, not as a group of uncoordinated, competing colleges regarding fundraising. He is placing a lot of responsibility on the vice president for development, but he is also giving her new resources and,
equally as important, the authority she has lacked in previous years.
The campus community will immediately realize that she has his support. In this option, Porter is convinced that the autonomy of the college deans cannot continue and must be changed. If the university is to
present a united approach in its fundraising efforts, a centralized and
closely coordinated program must be in place. The president knows
he has the support of his own board of trustees in taking this action,
and he is confident that there is no reason to delay what he knows is
the right thing to do!

QUESTIONS THAT MAY AID IN THE DISCUSSION
OF THIS CASE STUDY

1. Potential major donors are attracted to helping institutions accomplish their goals, especially in areas where they believe their funds can make an important difference in advancing new discoveries, service to others, and improving the quality of education. In thinking about Stantowne University, how can President Porter identify the most promising areas for attracting private donations? How does he prepare himself to "sell" these to prospective donors?
2. In the first 6 months of his presidency at Stantowne, how Anton Porter proceeds with this major issue will largely define his leadership style to the faculty, administration, alumni, students, and governing board. By his own definition, he is a "results-oriented" leader. Should his approach to this issue reflect a collegiate, consultative, or directive style? Can he somehow combine parts of all three styles?
3. Because many donors have specific giving interests that may re- late to only one academic program at the university (e.g., endowing a program in film studies), can a centralized fundraising program be effectively organized to meet such individually tailored interests?
4. The college deans have enjoyed autonomy in fundraising for years and believe this model is the most effective in achieving their goals. President Porter may encounter vigorous opposition to any new organizational plan that takes away most of their fundraising authority. Is this an issue so important that some of the college deans may resign from their positions because of their objections to the president's actions? If so, is it worth the risk?

Suggested Readings Related to This Case

Duderstadt, James J. (2007). *The View from the Helm: Leading the American University During an Era of Change.* Ann Arbor: University of Michigan Press. 2007

Kerr, Clark, (1985). *Presidents Make a Difference: Strengthening Leadership in Colleges and Universities.* Washington, DC: Association of Governing Boards of Universities and Colleges.

Kouzes, James M., & Posner, Barry Z. (1993). *Credibility: How Leaders Gain and Lose It, Why People Demand It.* San Francisco: Jossey Bass.

Preston, Caroline. (2009. September 17). Expert Advice for Donors. *The Chronicle of Philanthropy.*

FUNDING PSYCHOLOGICAL SUPPORT SERVICES AT MASTERTOWN UNIVERSITY

SUMMARY OF THE CASE

With growing demand for psychological services, the institution is finding it difficult to meet student needs with its existing resources. Moreover, the problems that students are presenting at this academically competitive university are increasingly serious and include substance abuse, relationship violence, and depression. In the past 6 months, the campus was shocked to learn of two suicides that occurred within its residence halls. There is an active alumni association and a parents council, and public concern is being expressed about the quality and amount of support services available to students. Although the counseling center staff has been increased by two new staff in the past 5 years, student demand now far exceeds the resources of the staff to respond to student needs. The counseling center director and the vice president for student affairs are expected to resolve this problem. However, in the current depressed economic situation, there are few attractive alternatives.

A DESCRIPTION OF MASTERTOWN UNIVERSITY

Mastertown University was founded in 1878 by a group of Methodist clergymen who desired to serve the needs of Eastern Kentucky by providing religious training and education to the growing region. After many years of limited enrollments and financial struggles, Mastertown emerged as a very successful college after becoming the fortunate recipient of some substantial gifts during the 1920s. Due to the visionary leadership of three presidents between

1935 and 1970, Mastertown's endowment grew significantly, and the institution became quite competitive, attracting excellent students from almost every state and an outstanding faculty. In the past 40 years, Mastertown's academic reputation has continued to grow, and reflecting its expanded graduate and research programs, it changed its name to "university" in 1975.

Mastertown's current president is John Horton, a chemist who served as president of another independent university for 7 years when he was recruited to the position by Mastertown's board of trustees. He was hired in 2007, at a time when the economic future looked bright for the institution. Mastertown's governing board is aggressive and was pleased to attract Horton as its new president because he seemed to possess the ability to move the institution into the top ranks of independent universities in the country. Indeed, Horton took the position because he saw outstanding opportunities to create new academic programs, build new facilities, and expand the research program.

When the Great Recession of 2008 occurred, the impact on Mastertown was serious. Within a period of only 9 months, the value of the institution's endowment decreased by more than 25 percent, and several major donors indicated that they would not be able to make their gifts as planned. Many of the plans that President Horton, his staff, and the governing board had for the future had to be set aside or delayed.

When President Horton came to Mastertown in 2007, he hired a new provost and a new student affairs vice president, both coming from other institutions. The new provost is Angela Fleming, a historian who had been Dean of Arts and Sciences at a similarly competitive independent institution in Texas. Her hiring was considered a major achievement by Mastertown because she is a dynamic educational leader. The new vice president for student affairs is Bob Gold, who had worked in the same position for President Horton at his previous institution for 5 years. Gold is well respected in the student affairs field and has the full confidence of President Horton. Both Gold and Fleming were highly enthusiastic about the opportunity to come to Mastertown and to work for Horton. Now, with the dire economic situation they are facing at the institution, they are not so sure they made a good decision.

THE STUDENTS AND THE FACULTY

Mastertown University enrolls 10,400 students. Of these, 8,000 are undergraduates and 2,400 are graduate students. The students come from almost every state, and some 45 countries are represented among its 350 international students. Almost 30 percent of the students are minorities, with Asian Americans, Hispanic/Latino Americans, and African Americans the most numerous. Most of the students come from upper middle-class backgrounds, although since 1992, Mastertown has aggressively recruited academically talented students from much more modest economic backgrounds almost entirely through providing financial assistance from its own endowment. Mastertown is not an inexpensive university; a yearly budget for an undergraduate comes to $44,500. The academic background of the student body is impressive, with 95 percent of the freshmen scoring in the top 10 percent of the national SAT tests.

Student life at Mastertown centers on the campus because most of the undergraduates live in residence halls, cooperative houses, and fraternity and sorority houses. The great majority of students who choose to attend Mastertown graduate after 4 years, and there is no retention problem. However, due to the competitive nature of the institution and the high achievement backgrounds of the students, the level of stress is high, and this is evidenced by substantial alcohol abuse, some relationship violence, and a high demand for medical and psychological services. A casual observer of student life might easily conclude that the students are attractive, active, and happy. Although this may be true in many cases, the number of "walking wounded" in the student body is substantial and a matter of growing concern for the institution.

Mastertown enjoys a beautiful campus and is located in a city of about 120,000 residents. Relationships with the city have been generally positive, but since President Horton came to Mastertown, some city-elected officials have expressed concern about his plans for expansion into some sensitive city neighborhoods. However, since the economic downturn, this concern has dissipated. Because the Mastertown students are active socially, some city residents have not been pleased with excessive drinking by students on weekends in the downtown area, sometimes resulting in disturbances and arrests. Students actively support Mastertown's athletic teams despite their rather mediocre records over the years.

Perhaps even more impressive than the academic quality of the students at Mastertown is the quality of the faculty. Due to the institution's substantial endowment and its high tuition, Mastertown has been able to remain competitive with other leading independent universities in attracting and retaining nationally outstanding faculty. Facilities and support for research are outstanding, and expectations for faculty productivity are high. Faculty are attracted to Mastertown for the academic prestige of the institution, the opportunities to advance within their discipline, and the pleasant nature of the campus and community. Reflecting their own high achievement, faculty at Mastertown are committed to their teaching and expect excellence from their students. The economic recession that began in 2008 came as a surprise to most of the faculty, who thought Mastertown was financially well off enough to not be affected by this downturn. There have been no new faculty hired in the past 2 years and no salary increases. The Faculty Senate is active and mostly supportive of the provost and president, but in the current economic uncertainty, many faculty members at Mastertown are mainly concerned about their own future. There is also a serious concern about the future directions the university will take.

THE ISSUE FOR THIS CASE STUDY

The issue for this case study is to find ways to address the health needs of the students at Mastertown University. The students are highly motivated to excel in everything they do, and in this competitive environment, they are experiencing considerable stress. This is evidenced too often in negative behaviors, depression, and even suicide. They are visiting the counseling center in record numbers, and the institution does not have sufficient professional staff in that facility to meet their needs. Moreover, the university's financial condition has deteriorated since the 2008 recession, giving it fewer options to respond with more resources in support of students.

Student Affairs Vice President Gold is fully aware of the problem of not being able to provide adequate resources in support of the psychological needs of Mastertown students. He is also aware of the serious consequences to students who cannot get the help they need. He has met frequently with the counseling center staff and has worked closely with them. He has also made President Horton and Provost Fleming familiar with the problem. While receiving understanding and concern, he has not been successful in securing additional staff or financial resources for the counseling center. Gold is keenly aware of the difficult financial situation facing the university and shares the concern of other administrators and faculty that substantial cutbacks and layoffs may be imminent. But he knows it is his responsibility to do everything he can to provide needed psychological services, and he knows the negative consequences of ignoring the problem.

SOME OPTIONS FOR ADDRESSING THE ISSUE

1. Vice President Gold should work to convince the president and provost that the existing mandatory health fee of $450 per year per student should be increased to $750 in order to provide the needed additional psychological services. With the additional monies, adequate resources would be available to hire an additional six licensed counseling psychologists at the counseling center. The Center now has a staff of 12 licensed counseling psychologists.

This option, of course, would earmark an increased fee and quickly provide the dollars needed to address this serious problem. However, increasing the already high tuition of $31,000 per year per student by another $300 will not prove popular with students or their parents. The institution has already reduced its endowment due to increased financial needs of the students. Gold faces a substantial challenge in seeking the approval of the Mastertown University student government association, which has a historically important role in expressing its views about new student fee assessments. The student affairs VP also knows he will have to be persuasive with President Horton and Provost Fleming and cannot proceed without their approval. He knows the governing board is aware of the problem, but of course it is the president's decision about whether to recommend such a fee increase to the board. Moreover, his colleague, Provost Fleming, is under considerable pressure by the faculty, who feel their own needs are not being addressed by the institution during this difficult time. Finally, Gold is being pressed by his own student affairs staff, who are working each day with students who are experiencing serious personal problems in their lives.

2. Vice President Gold should convince President Horton that a blue ribbon, campus-wide task force of students, faculty, and alumni should be appointed to address this issue and to make recommendations for resolving it. Given 4 to 5 months to meet and discuss all aspects of this issue, such a task force might give needed visibility to the issue and establish it as a top priority for the university.

This option, although not immediately solving the problem, may extend the concern beyond the division of student affairs and result in more campus-wide support for resolving the issue. However, the provost and her faculty may be likely to oppose giving such a high priority to this issue at such a critical financial time at the institution. The provost may logically ask, "What about faculty salaries or needed research support in order to compete for external funds?" Some students and faculty may be highly skeptical of such a special task force, suggesting that it has obviously been created as a "straw man" to justify what the student affairs vice president already knows he is going to do. Finally, President Horton may be wary of the recommendations such a task force may publicly present, potentially producing negative publicity on the university, especially when there are insufficient resources to support what the task force is likely to suggest.

3. Vice President Gold, who has responsibility for eight other departments within the student affairs division, should require the transfer of six full-time professional staff to the counseling center to increase the Center's capability to address the personal problems of students. Staff from the dean of students office, the advising center, the housing office, and the career services office will be recruited for this purpose.

This option, while quickly adding more staff to the counseling center, may disrupt other offices in the student affairs division, no less the professional careers of the six staff being "recruited" for the purpose. Because none of these transferred staff is a licensed counseling psychologist, they will obviously have to be closely supervised by the existing staff of the counseling center and will not be able to deal with the most seriously disturbed students. But taking such bold action may convince the president and provost that Vice President Gold is willing to address this serious problem within his own division without asking for additional funds and may enhance his role within the administration of Mastertown University. The transferred staff may only be a temporary "solution" for a period of 2 to 3 years, when it is hoped that the financial condition of the institution may improve. Of course, there may be a substantial objection on the part of the existing licensed counseling psychologists in the counseling center to having to supervise staff they consider untrained for such an assignment.

4. Vice President Gold should convince the counseling center staff to set strict limits on the number of sessions they have with individual students, requiring the staff to refer more serious cases to private practitioners in the city. This could free up more time to see more students but not for extended periods of time. Moreover, Gold should invite selected private counseling psychologists to offer their services to students by providing space in the Mastertown University counseling center, thus extending the services to students. Students would be billed for the fees that these private practitioners would charge but at a negotiated, lower rate than they would pay off campus.

The student affairs vice president is likely to hear vigorous objections to the idea of limiting the number of visits a student can have with a counselor. But he asserts that no institution can afford such intensive, long term individual care for substantial numbers of students, and he knows that a counselor can see more students if not tied down with several students who come in for assistance every week during the academic year. It is also highly likely that students will object to paying what they consider unfair charges for counseling they have previously received for free from their university. This option, of course, has the advantage of Vice President Gold taking a strong action within his own division to address the problem without depending on or requesting support from the president or provost.

QUESTIONS THAT MAY AID IN THE DISCUSSION
OF THIS CASE STUDY

1. Vice President Gold has the advantage of being secure in his relationship with President Horton, with whom he has worked before at another institution. Thus, he does not have to second guess the president, and he can be quite confident that the president will respond favorably to what he feels is best for the institution and its students. But Gold has not had such a history with Provost Fleming, and he knows the provost is the "first among equals" in the administrative structure of the university. To what extent is the support of the provost essential for Gold in each of the alternative "solutions?" Can he be successful without her support? If so, what are some ways he can earn her support?

2. If Gold decides to pursue the appointment of the campus-wide task force to address this issue, will he be perceived as a weak and bureaucratic administrator who is reluctant to make tough decisions? Or is such an option a wise and necessary tactic to build greater acceptance and understanding of the problem?

3. Can Gold continue to earn the respect and support of the student body if he imposes an additional fee on their tuition over their certain objections? How important is it for the senior student affairs administrator to act on what students say they want or will support? Can Gold be an effective advocate for student needs at Mastertown University and at the same time make decisions that the students do not support?

4. How risky is it for Gold to disrupt the staff in his own division by essentially reassigning professional staff and, in effect, declaring the counseling center as the most important priority among the nine departments in the division? Is he placing the accreditation of the counseling center in jeopardy by transferring nonlicensed staff to assist students facing problems in their lives? What preparation will be required with the department heads to make this transfer of staff work, and what follow-up will be needed?

5. By suggesting that students visiting the counseling center be charged a fee when they see an "outside" counselor, is Gold taking a risky step that may encourage others in the administration to place the entire counseling center on a fee-for-services status? Will students

actually show up and pay these charges, or will they stay away, thus worsening an already serious mental health situation on the campus?

Suggested Readings Related to this Case

Archer, James, Jr., & Cooper, Stewart. (1998). *Counseling and Mental Health Services on Campus: A Handbook of Contemporary Practices and Challenges.* San Francisco: Jossey-Bass.

Benton, Sherry A., & Benton, Stephen L. (2006). *College Student Mental Health: Effective Services and Strategies Across Campus.* Washington, DC: NASPA. 2006.

Dunkle, John H. (Ed.). (2009). *Dealing with Behavioral and Psychological Problems of Students: A Contemporary Update. New Directions for Student Services.* Washington, DC: NASPA.

Kadison, Richard, & Theresa Kay Geronimo. (2005). *College of the Overwhelmed: The College Mental Health Crisis and What to Do About It.* San Francisco: Jossey Bass.

RETHINKING BECKINGTOWN COLLEGE'S FINANCIAL AID POLICY

SUMMARY OF THE CASE

Beckingtown College is a small, prestigious liberal arts institution located in the upper Midwest. It was founded in 1855 and is highly selective in admissions. The college's endowment increased to $3.5 billion in 2005, making it one of the richest colleges in the country in relation to the size of its student body. As a result of its successful fundraising efforts and wise investment policy, the college's board of trustees decided in 2006 that it had the ability to use its substantial endowment to achieve greater economic diversity in the student body. Due to the high cost of attending Beckingtown, the students overwhelmingly come from affluent families. The college trustees want to attract bright students from less affluent families, increase the ethnic diversity of the student body, and make it possible for disadvantaged students to graduate from the college without debt. In 2006, the board of trustees, at the recommendation of the college's president, announced that any student coming from a family with $50,000 annual income or lower would be able to attend the college and graduate debt free after 4 years. The college would use income from its endowment to fund this aid program. The effort to attract such students began at once. But when the economic recession of 2008 happened, the value of the college's endowment decreased by more than $650 million. It is now 2010. Although the college is pleased with the program's success, the board of trustees has to decide what the future of the program will be. The board has asked the president for his recommendations.

A DESCRIPTION OF BECKINGTOWN COLLEGE

Beckingtown College is located in a small town of 12,000 people and is annually listed in a popular magazine as among the 10 best small liberal arts colleges in the United States. It attracts superior students from throughout the country and has a distinguished faculty. It does not offer graduate programs and prides itself on high-quality teaching.

The college has kept its enrollment at 1,800 students for many years, convinced this size is ideal for enabling it to accomplish its academic goals. Its curriculum is rigorous and emphasizes individual study with faculty and provides many opportunities for students to engage in research. The college has outstanding programs in biological science, mathematics, and chemistry, and many of its graduates go on to medical school and graduate study in the sciences.

As an indication of the excellence of the academic program at Beckingtown College, 24 of its students have been selected as Rhodes Scholars since 1938, and 74 of its students have been selected as Fulbright Scholars since 1949. There is great pride in the college, and alumni support is among the best in the nation, measured both by percentage of graduates who give money to the college each year and by the total amount given.

For the past 15 years, the faculty and administration of the college have required all students to participate in an international educational experience, and the college supports exchange programs in Europe, Asia, and Africa. The college also insists that its students complete intensive study of another language before graduation.

One of the college's graduates was a U.S. president, 6 have been U.S. senators, and 11 have been governors of various states. Beckingtown College has emphasized public service to its students for decades, and many of its outstanding faculty have served in governmental positions at the state and national levels.

Beckingtown College's endowment is largely the result of the leadership of three presidents, who, after World War II ended, recognized the importance of a substantial endowment in order for the college to compete for the best faculty and students and also to build and maintain outstanding academic facilities. These presidents became active fundraisers and hired excellent investment advisers. The college's endowment continued to grow and increased dramatically beginning in about 1990. Members of the board of trustees have been very successful in managing and contributing to the endowment, and several of its members are well known and highly successful corporate executives and investors.

The president of Beckingtown College is Robert Stanfield, a historian who has been in his position for 8 years. He was previously the chief academic officer at another prestigious liberal arts college in the Northeast.

Everyone associated with the college is strongly committed to academic excellence and public service, and the institution is justifiably proud of its record. It knows it must continue to work hard to attract and retain its outstanding students and faculty in order to maintain its position as one of the most admired liberal arts colleges in the country.

THE STUDENTS AND THE FACULTY

The students at Beckingtown College come from every state in the country and, in 2010, from 24 foreign countries as well. All of the students had superior academic and extracurricular records in their secondary schools and consider themselves fortunate to be at Beckingtown, as there were 4,500 applications for the 410 spaces in the 2010 freshmen class. The college strives to maintain a 50–50 ratio of men and women. Almost 20 percent of the entering students attended private high schools, and many were attracted to Beckingtown for the opportunity to become a member of one of its intercollegiate athletic teams. With 12 sports for men and 13 for women, more than half of the college's students participate on the teams.

The cost of attending the college is high–$49,000 per year. Despite the affluence of most of the students' families, almost 30 percent of the students are recipients of some kind of financial aid, mostly in loans. These students graduate with an average of $45,000 in loan obligations.

Although the students are not pushed by the faculty to select an academic major in their first 2 years at the college, most students decide to concentrate their studies in one or two subjects by their third year.

In 2010, the most popular academic majors were biology, chemistry, psychology, and mathematics. Most of the college's graduates continue their education after leaving Beckingtown, and the college is well known for the large number of students who are accepted at leading law and medical schools around the country and also in outstanding graduate programs.

Students form a variety of social, academic, musical, recreational, religious, and political organizations at the college, and, in recent years, there has been a big increase in service activities as well. Beckingtown students have enjoyed their reputation for "creative humor" for many years, and there is a tradition of harmless but imaginative pranks among competing student groups.

Beckingtown College has not been as successful as it would like to be in attracting minority students to the institution. Despite quite generous scholarship support, only about 7 percent of its student body consists of minorities. This continues to be a matter of concern to President Stanfield and the faculty.

Most of the students live in campus residence halls and academic theme houses, and junior faculty members and other staff members also live in these facilities as residence advisers. Close faculty–student relationships are the norm at the college, and sometimes students complain that there is "no place to hide" at the college because everyone knows one another!

All of the students participate in some form of international study during their years at the college. Faculty are also active participants and advisers in the various study-abroad experiences the students have. Each academic year, one of the liveliest and most enjoyable college wide seminars takes place on a weekend when students, returning from their study overseas, share their experiences.

The faculty at Beckingtown College are outstanding scholars and teachers who have been attracted to the institution for its excellent academic reputation, the high quality of the students, the competitive salaries, and the opportunities for continuing professional development. The college has been selective in hiring new faculty, and faculty who earn tenure at Beckingtown are among the most outstanding scholars in their academic disciplines.

Faculty know that they hold privileged academic appointments at the college and want to remain there for the attractive opportunities they have. They are strongly committed to teaching undergraduates and serving as mentors for the students.

Most faculty also have their own research programs and, because of the financial assets of the college, are provided with ample support for their work with good labs and a fine library, along with regular sabbaticals.

There is a college senate at Beckingtown College, and its 24 faculty members are elected by their colleagues for 3-year terms. The senate also includes three students and three college staff. The senate is known for its lively and sometimes humorous debates, but it is serious about its important role in serving the college and advancing its academic programs. The senate has a long tradition of reviewing college policies, proposing new programs, and advising the president of the college.

Beckingtown College has a long tradition of close faculty–student relationships, and much of its graduates' success has been attributed to this tradition. Faculty are strongly committed to the value of public service and participate with their students in a variety of projects during the year in the community, region, and nation. The college is considered one of the national leaders in service learning and volunteer community service.

THE ISSUE TO BE ADDRESSED IN THIS STUDY

As Beckingtown College continued to prosper, become annually recognized nationally for its academic excellence, and attract outstanding students, the college's board of trustees, at the behest of the college president, Robert Stanfield, debated the future direction of the institution. The college was pleased with its many assets but strongly felt that it had a "social and moral obligation" to serve a greater economic diversity of students. It did not want to become an elitist college only for the wealthy, and it wanted to serve the nation and world by becoming a college where superior students could attend and graduate regardless of their families' ability to pay.

To meet its goal of attracting high-performing students from modest financial backgrounds, the board of trustees decided to make a major financial commitment to any admitted student from a family whose income was less than $50,000 per year so that the student could attend and graduate from Beckingtown College with no debt. The board estimated that, just for one student, this financial obligation would total some $100,000 for his or her undergraduate education. But with a growing endowment of more than $3.5 billion, the college was earning more than $100 million per year in interest alone. Moreover, during the past 7 years, the endowment itself increased in value by at least 7 percent per year. Thus, the board of trustees set a goal for itself to support as many as 350 students eventually in this "graduate with no debt" program. President Stanfield was pleased with the board's support of his proposal and immediately instructed his admissions and financial aid office to begin implementing the program.

The college was not the first highly prestigious, selective institution to adopt this "no debt" program, and Beckingtown was aware that four of its competitor institutions had adopted this policy 2 years earlier. But its commitment to the program is sincere, and the college is convinced this is the right thing to do. Moreover, when President Stanfield presented this proposal to the college senate, the reaction of the faculty, staff, and students was positive. The college did hear from some worried alumni, who are concerned that their children, who want to attend Beckingtown College, may be "discriminated" against on the basis of family income.

The new program was put in place beginning in the fall semester of 2006, and the college was pleased that 30 freshmen in the class of 420 qualified for it. The college looked forward to admitting even more students in the program the next year, and admissions staff reported increased interest in attending the college among outstanding students from modest financial backgrounds. The college also was pleased that it received a good deal of positive coverage and acclaim for this program in the media.

This program has been so successful at Beckingtown College that members of the college senate and others have urged President Stanfield and the board of trustees to increase the number of students in it. In 2010, the number of students at the college in the program grew to 180, still short of the eventual goal of 350, but nevertheless headed in a positive direction. The first students admitted to the program graduated, debt free, in June 2010.

When the Great Recession of 2008 erupted on the U.S. and world economy, the president and board of trustees were devastated when they learned how quickly and severely the impact was on the value of the college's endowment. After years of positive growth, the $3.5 billion endowment decreased in value to $2.4 billion in less than 14 months! It was obvious to the president and board of trustees that some serious decisions would have to be made at the college that would affect its academic programs, its faculty and students, and its plans to build and upgrade some of its physical facilities. One of the programs in jeopardy was the very popular "no debt at graduation" program started only 4 years ago at Beckingtown College. The board of trustees has asked President Stanfield for a plan to address this problem and to present it to the board in the next 2 months.

President Stanfield is fully aware of the problems and, of course, anticipated the board's request. He has been working with his staff on it for several weeks already. Here are some options he is considering.

SOME OPTIONS FOR ADDRESSING THIS ISSUE

1. Given the expensive nature of this program and the dire financial issues facing the college, President Stanfield should convince the board of trustees to announce that the program will be discontinued when the currently enrolled students have graduated, which will be in 2013. The college's commitments to these students will be honored. The announcement will also include an assurance that the program may be reinstated if and when the college's financial situation improves. The president and board are facing a variety of serious issues at the college because of the big decrease in the value of the endowment, such as frozen faculty and staff salaries, delayed construction of needed academic facilities, and pressure from students and their families not to increase tuition. The "no debt" program has gained the institution a good deal of positive publicity, and the college and its board of trustees believe it is the right thing to do, but the college simply cannot afford it any longer, and it must be terminated.

President Stanfield is pained by having to make this decision. He knows when it is announced, it will not reflect positively on the college and, worse, some students who had dreamed of attending Beckingtown College will be deprived of the opportunity. He believes it is important that his college not become accessible only by students from affluent families. He is still stunned by how quickly and drastically the college was impacted by the economic recession. Although he is aware that his competitor colleges around the country have been similarly affected, he knows that it is his responsibility to make the difficult decisions that will enable the college to maintain its academic excellence. After seeing some positive advancements at the college in his first years as president, when almost anything seemed possible, he now faces some daunting challenges.

2. President Stanfield, despite the serious damage done to the college's financial situation, still has many resources at his disposal, and he is determined to find a way to keep the "no debt" program alive. He is known as an upbeat and positive leader, and he knows there is a large amount of good will and loyalty among the college's supporters and alumni. He believes he can tap into this good will, even during a time of economic trouble in the country, by announcing a special $1 billion "campaign for Beckingtown." He knows this bold plan will require the board of trustees' support as well as the college's Foundation board and that many people will be very skeptical of such a plan. But, President Stanfield argues, there is a long tradition of support for the college, and he believes that there are many wealthy alumni and friends of the college who will respond positively to the college they love. The president's campaign, announced in the fall of 2010, will have a target date of 2014. Given the circumstances with the economy, President Stanfield feels this is no time to allow Beckingtown College to back away from the challenges it must face in order to maintain its commitment to academic excellence. If the campaign is successful, the president will continue the "no debt" program so dear to his heart.

The president knows he is taking a big risk with this option, but he feels if he does nothing, the college will decline in quality and prestige. At a time when he sees other institutions, both public and private, laying off faculty and staff, terminating various academic programs, and stopping needed construction projects, President Stanfield feels a better strategy is to buck this trend and aggressively seek donor support. He knows the great attachment that alumni have to the college, and he also is aware that many of them are prominent, successful, and wealthy individuals. He is betting his own future and that of the college on this special campaign. He is determined to push the college to meet this financial challenge and to restore the "no debt" program.

3. The "no debt" program has gained excellent support within Beckingtown College, and President Stanfield knows any decision to change the program will be met with many challenges. He believes in the long-time tradition of collegial decision making, and he knows the faculty, staff, students, and alumni will expect to be involved in any consideration of the future of this program. Thus, in this option, the president decides to speak to the college senate, where he will describe in detail the financial challenges the college is facing and discuss the success the "no debt" program has had, and how important it is in the college's goal to serve a broader range of students. He will also ask for the college senate's support in his decision to appoint a special college-wide task force, whose assignment it will be to study this issue and make its recommendations to him and the senate in the next 8 weeks. The task force will include six faculty, three students, two staff, and two alumni. It will be chaired by a highly respected faculty member who retired from the college just 2 years ago after having taught at Beckingtown for 32 years.

In this option, the president is affirming the college's long tradition of campus-wide governance, trusting the academic community to deal thoughtfully with this important issue. He is also aware that, without the support of faculty, students, staff, and alumni, any decision made concerning the future of the program will be criticized. Further, he knows that the college senate and others are not used to dealing with issues where serious constraints about money are central—in recent years, Beckingtown College has always had sufficient funds that issues could be addressed purely on the basis of the attractiveness of the program. By taking this option, the president is trusting the college governance process and is assuming that the task force and college senate will present a workable and realistic set of recommendations. However, he knows he may have to reject what they suggest if it places the college in an unacceptable financial situation.

4. President Stanfield is concerned about the many financial issues the college is facing. He knows that cutbacks will have to be made in some areas, that faculty and staff salaries will have to be frozen, that student tuition cannot be raised, and that construction projects on campus will have to be delayed. However, in this option, the president decides that the "no debt" program should be maintained. He is committed to it because he feels it is the right thing to do, and he also feels that if it were eliminated, it would reflect poorly on the college's prestige and reputation. He knows that the college's endowment has taken a serious hit; however, he also is confident that the financial markets will rebound and that the endowment is sufficiently large that the college can continue this program without doing serious, long-term damage to it. Thus, he decides to approach the board of trustees with his recommendation that the program be maintained in its current form.

By taking this action, President Stanfield is counting on his board of trustees to confirm its support for him and its confidence in him. He knows this is a bold step, and, of course, he is betting on his ability to convince his board that this is the right thing to do. He understands the risks involved, especially if the financial markets do not improve, and the college endowment decreases in value in the next 2 to 3 years. In light of some of his counterpart institutions announcing that they are dropping their "no debt" programs, the president feels Beckingtown College can place itself in a better competitive position by maintaining its program. By doing so, the president hopes his decision to continue the "no debt" program will result in the enthusiastic support and pride among the colleges' constituents.

QUESTIONS THAT MAY AID IN THE DISCUSSION
OF THIS CASE STUDY

1. Is President Stanfield placing too much emphasis on this "no debt" program at his college at a time when there are more important problems caused by the financial crisis?
2. As part of Option 4, would it be wiser to continue the program but cut the numbers of students recruited by 50 percent or drop the

absolute "no debt" aspect at graduation and cap a maximum debt total for the affected students at $30,000?

3. The college has enjoyed wonderful and loyal support from its alumni and friends for many years. In Option 2, where a new fundraising campaign is the strategy, what are the consequences of failing to meet the goals of such a campaign? Is it worth the risk?

4. Even if the "no debt" program can be maintained, the overwhelming majority of the student body will still come from affluent families given the high costs of attending the college. Are there other realistic alternatives for the college to become more accessible to less affluent students?

Suggested Readings Related to This Case

Bowen, Howard G., Bok, Derek, & Loury, Glenn C. (2000). *The Shape of the River.* *Princeton*, NJ: Princeton University Press.

Hoover, Eric. (2007, July 27). Amherst College Replaces Loans with Grants, Joining Princeton and Davidson. *The Chronicle of Higher Education.*

The College Board. (2009). *Getting Financial Aid 2010.* New York: Author.

Wilkinson, Rupert. (2005). *Aiding Students, Buying Students: Financial Aid in America.* Nashville, TN. Vanderbilt University Press.

A FUNDRAISING DILEMMA AT PACKHURST COLLEGE

SUMMARY OF THE CASE

Packhurst College is a private institution in the Midwest and enrolls 2,400 undergraduate students. It was founded in 1875 by four Protestant ministers. The college has an excellent academic reputation and attracts students from more than 25 states. It has a fairly modest endowment of $35 million, and its president, Anne Seger, has been in her position for 6 years. As Packhurst's president, she knows the board of trustees expects her to be active in fundraising and to increase the value of the college's endowment. In 1959, Packhurst College, in recognition of its expanding academic mission, decided to sever its formal affiliation with the church. Now, in 2010, President Seger is confronted with a dilemma with a major donor, whose proposed gift has the potential to transform the college but has placed the president and the college in an uncomfortable position.

A DESCRIPTION OF PACKHURST COLLEGE

Packhurst College is located in a small town of 10,000 residents in the Midwest. Founded by a small and dedicated group of Protestant ministers determined to establish a college to train clergy for the region, it struggled to survive for many years, managing to continue mainly through the support of the national church organization. Its enrollment did not exceed 150 until after 1910, and it finally reached almost 400 by 1933. However, the impact of the Great Depression and World War II almost caused the college to close, and the enrollment was only 150 in 1945. But the boom in enrollment that occurred at so many colleges after the war, together with the dynamic leadership of John Lansing, Packhurst's president at the time, enabled the college to flourish. By 1955, the college had grown to 1,100 students, had expanded its curriculum, and had significantly upgraded its faculty.

As Packhurst College continued to grow, its academic reputation was also enhanced. The college attracted students from outside the Midwest, and admissions became quite selective. John Lansing's successor was hired in 1957 from another private college in the Northeast, and he was successful in creating the Packhurst College Foundation and began seeking outside funds to build an endowment for the college. The creation of the Foundation was not viewed positively by the national church organization affiliated with Packhurst, and the relationship between the college and the church organization became sufficiently tense that in, 1959, the college decided to sever its affiliation with the church. Its objective was to become a truly independent and more diverse college and felt its long-time identification with the church was hindering its development. This was a momentous decision, but fears on the part of some trustees and faculty that the college would lose support, especially from its alumni, were not realized. The college continued to grow and flourish, and in 1985 the board of trustees decided to cap the college's enrollment at 2,200. The college now wants to expand its curriculum to provide more extensive work in the sciences and to attract a more diverse student body.

Since the college's foundation was established in 1957, all succeeding presidents and the board of trustees continued to build the college's endowment, and by 2010 it had reached $35 million. However, the current president, Anne Seger, and the governing board recognized that this endowment is modest given the academic aspirations and needs of the college, especially in the areas of facilities and student support. Moreover, President Seger is keenly aware that four other private colleges in the region, all competitors of Packhurst, have endowments of more than $200 million. She is spending more and more of her time away from the campus, talking with potential donors and cultivating support for the college.

Packhurst has enjoyed loyal support from its alumni, especially those who have graduated since the 1950s. The alumni are reasonably generous with annual donations to their Alma Mater, although the bulk of the endowment has been the result of gifts from individuals not formally affiliated with the college and from selected corporations.

The Packhurst College Foundation board of directors consists of 50 outstanding volunteers, about half of whom are alumni. The college's director of development was hired by President Seger and reports directly to her. The development staff has expanded to 15 full-time professionals, reflecting President Seger's and the governing board's goals to enhance the endowment. The college is painfully aware that the current economic recession has made their effort to obtain major gifts a difficult challenge.

THE STUDENTS AND THE FACULTY

The current students at Packhurst are the most academically talented the college has ever attracted. They come from more than 25 states, although most of them come from within the state and from three adjacent states. For the freshman class of 2010, the college selected 475 students from 1,600 applicants, and most of the newly enrolled students were in the top third of their high school classes and in the top half of all students taking the SAT exam. The students mostly live on campus in residence halls and Greek houses, and they come mostly from middle- and upper middle-class families. The annual cost to attend Packhurst is $39,000, which is about average for private colleges in the region.

Students' academic interests have shifted in recent years, with biology, chemistry, and business administration becoming the most popular majors. Enrollment in the social sciences and humanities is fairly steady, but the number of students expressing interest in teaching has decreased significantly. Almost 30 percent of Packhurst students go on to professional and graduate schools after completing their studies.

Student life at the college is active, reflecting the residential nature of the institution. Students enjoy the small town where the college is located and are quite involved in service activities in the area. Although the social life can become noisy, relationships between the college and the local community have remained fairly cordial and trusting. More than 80 percent of the students who begin their studies at Packhurst graduate within 4 years, and others usually stay until they complete their studies.

Minorities comprise only about 6 percent of the student body at Packhurst, and the college has not been as successful in its efforts to expand ethnic diversity in recent years. This is a matter of serious concern to President Seger, the faculty, and the board of trustees, and they recognize that the rural, small town location of the college may be a challenge, as well as the relatively high cost of attendance, especially in comparison with the five public universities within the state. The college recognizes that, to become more diverse, it will need significantly increased funds from its own endowment to compete in financial aid for students.

The faculty at Packhurst has changed in the past several years; it is much more diverse and academically sophisticated than it was 25 years ago. The faculty is fairly young and was specifically recruited to the college because of its commitment to undergraduate teaching. However, many of the current faculty are also interested in research, and many are scholars who contribute to the advancement of their academic disciplines. Most faculty enjoy their work at Packhurst, although the salaries at the college are below that of their competitor institutions, a matter well known by President Seger and the board of trustees. Faculty have become more and more unhappy with the salary situation, and the president and board recognize that some of its best faculty may leave the college for better paying positions at other institutions if improvements cannot be made. Given the current economic conditions, however, the college is extremely reluctant to raise its tuition, for fear of losing students, and knows that its endowment is not sufficient to bolster faculty salaries.

Faculty are involved in virtually every area of campus governance at Packhurst, and this longstanding tradition of collegiality is treasured by them. The faculty senate is a lively and active "debating society" at Packhurst, which engages in everything from the curriculum, hiring of administrators, facilities, tuition, and college athletics. In recent years, the senate has focused much of its attention on the college budget and has urged the president and the board of trustees to continue to expand its fundraising efforts for the college. There has always been some tension between the president and the faculty senate, but for the most part, the president has been able to pursue her goals without undo interference from the senate.

THE ISSUE TO BE ADDRESSED IN THIS CASE STUDY

President Seger and one of the senior development officers at Packhurst have been holding regular visits with a wealthy alumnus of the college for the past 4 years. This alumnus lives in Chicago, and President Seger has invited him to the college for various events and occasions and has engaged him in conversations with key faculty and board of trustee members. The alumnus made his money primarily in the software and computer fields and is reportedly worth almost $1 billion. He is conservative in his political and religious views. While friendly and loyal to his Alma Mater, Packhurst College, he is privately quite critical of the college in his conversations with President Seger. The president does not share his views and has been patient and tolerant of this alumnus for years, hopeful that he will demonstrate his support for the college with a major gift while not openly trying to impose his political or religious views in any way.

President Seger has invited the alumnus to special lectures on campus, student dramatic performances, and a commencement exercise, where the alumnus was honored with the prestigious "Packhurst College Achievement Award." During the 4 years that President Seger and her senior development colleague have been cultivating the alumnus' interest in the college, they have not asked him for any specific gift. However, it is obvious that they are close to doing so, and the alumnus, being a sophisticated entrepreneur, is not naïve about this process.

The president feels she has established a mutual trust and respect with this alumnus and is hopeful that any differences they have might be resolved when he is finally ready to become a donor.

On a Monday morning in September 2010, President Seger receives an unexpected phone call from the alumnus, who asks her if she would be willing to come to Chicago and meet with him and to bring the college's attorney as well! He indicates that he has a serious proposal to discuss with her. She immediately makes arrangements to fly to Chicago for a meeting with the alumnus the next day.

In all the previous 50+ years of the college's fundraising efforts, the largest single gift was for $1 million from an elderly resident of the town who left her entire estate to the college. President Seger, aware of the ability of the current Chicago-based alumnus' financial assets, has never mentioned a figure to him, but she is privately hopeful that he might give as much as $5 million to the college, which would represent a tremendous opportunity for the college. Thus, when she met the alumnus in his office, she was absolutely stunned when he informed her that he was prepared to make a $60 million gift to the college! In her wildest dreams, she never could have imagined such a gift, and she knew it could propel the college into the next level of academic distinction and truly be transformative to the institution. Such a gift would almost triple the college endowment and would send a clear signal to the larger academic community that Packhurst College was on the move!

Despite the cordial and trusting relationship she had built with the alumnus during the past 4 years, President Seger was greatly taken aback when she was told by the alumnus that his proposed $60 million gift to the college was contingent on her assurance that the following three things would be accomplished: (1) all Packhurst College freshmen would be required to enroll in a year-long course in "Christian Ethics and Values," (2) the college should find a way to reaffiliate with the national church organization, and (3) special consideration in admissions should be given to students who are active members of the church. The alumnus was friendly but firm in his determination to accomplish these changes, which he sincerely feels are needed at the college and will strengthen its impact. President Seger was eager not to immediately rebuff this incredible offer, so she enthusiastically thanked the alumnus for his dedication to the college and told him that she needed to return to campus and get back to him soon with a formal response. Knowing the sensitive nature of this potential gift, she and the alumnus agreed to keep the matter completely confidential. However, she was already worried about the conditions the alumnus attached to his potential gift and knew that if these conditions became publicly known, it would result in considerable debate and, perhaps, the loss of this incredibly important gift to the college.

President Seger had an anxious trip back to her campus. Now she must consider how to proceed. The following represent some options she might pursue:

SOME OPTIONS FOR ADDRESSING THIS ISSUE

1. President Seger is so astounded over this proposed gift that she knows she needs some time to settle down and think about it! The amount of the proposed gift is such that it could literally transform the college. However, she also knows that she and the college cannot accept any gift that would be contingent on the college changing its policies, curriculum, or affiliations. To do so would be to compromise the very nature of the college and its academic integrity. The college has never accepted any gift that had such conditions attached to it. Moreover, President Seger knows that she must handle this matter on her own because if the potential gift and its conditions became public, it would result in negative publicity for the college and embarrassment for the wealthy donor. Thus, in this option, President Seger returns to Chicago later in the week, sincerely thanks the alumnus for his generous gesture, but firmly informs him that the college cannot accept the gift given the conditions he presented.

It is not every day that a college president rejects a $60 million gift from a wealthy and proud alumnus! By taking this action, President Seger has to feel confident that her board of trustees will support her actions especially because she has decided not to tell them about it before she rejects the gift. Given the volatility of the situation, she does not think she can keep the matter confidential if she shares it with her board; as a savvy president, she knows things have a way of leaking! The risk is too great in her mind. Moreover, she still holds out the possibility in her own mind that she might be able to convince the donor to remove the conditions he has set for the gift. She is also aware that if news about this gift were to become public, many college supporters might blame her for her losing it, denying the college the most significant opportunity since its founding.

2. President Seger is known as a persuasive, charming, and determined leader. She believes there has to be a way to obtain this gift for the college. In this option, she has a private, confidential conversation with the chair of her board of trustees, and they decide to contact the only living ex-president of the college and two prominent college alumni and make a trip back to Chicago to visit with the wealthy alumnus. This group, all well known by the alumnus, will meet with him, thank him for his wonderful gesture, and then try to persuade him that his gift could truly transform the college, but that the conditions he has set just cannot work. The ex-president appeals to the wealthy alumnus' loyalty to the values of the college, and the prominent alumni, both of whom are businessmen used to negotiation, try to point out how these conditions will actually hurt the college. The group is cordial and patient with the alumnus and assure him they do not need an immediate answer. They agree to continue the conversation, and the group indicates it would be willing to come to Chicago for another meeting if necessary.

In this option, President Seger is tapping into what she knows are the most respected and well-known representatives of the college to try to reason with the prospective donor. She is confident in their trust and feels reasonably sure that information about the potential gift and this Chicago meeting will not become public. Of course, she does not know what the wealthy alumnus in Chicago will do! While he was cordial in the meeting and did not seem to resent being visited by this distinguished delegation, she worried that perhaps he might get angry about being pressured and might decide to back away entirely from giving to the college. Or he might decide to go public with this situation and, in anger, "expose" the college for rejecting his gift because of its "unwillingness to teach values and ethics" to its students.

3. President Seger is a realist and knows that compromise is often the only effective way of resolving problems. She has been successful in her career in bringing together people who have strong disagreements on academic issues, and she knows that it is often necessary to give as well as take in negotiations. Thus, in this option, the president meets with her chair of the board of trustees and asks for permission to negotiate with the wealthy donor about the conditions he has set. She has spent 4 years meeting with this potential donor and feels she knows him well, and she also knows his strong personal views and commitments. After doing some investigation on her own, she thinks she can arrange a "cooperative exchange" between the church and the *college; that she can convince the faculty to include required reading and discussion about values and ethics in the required American Civilization course all freshmen must take, and high school students who are active members of the church will be encouraged to apply to the college. President Seger hopes that the wealthy alumnus might be satisfied with these revised conditions and that the faculty and other supporters of the college will accept and understand them. She believes that, by proposing such actions, she might forge an acceptable compromise, maintain the academic integrity of the college, and be successful in obtaining the $60 million gift!*

The president clearly knows this is a risky option. But she wants this gift for the college and feels it is worth compromising with the donor in order to obtain it. Of course, she doesn't know whether the donor might be willing to agree to any such compromise, but she is confident in her own ability to negotiate and discuss this with him. She is aware that such an approach may backfire, as her faculty and other college supporters may see it all as a sham and refuse to accept any part of the proposal. She is keenly aware that if this were to happen, her time as president of Packhurst College will certainly be over!

4. President Seger is an excellent reader of people. In the 4 years of cultivating this donor's interest in his Alma Mater, she has been patient and tolerant of his large ego. She also knows that he has already accomplished so much in his business activities that he is no longer primarily motivated by making money. She feels he is sincere in his effort to "do good things," but she is also convinced that he strongly desires public adulation and publicity for doing so. Thus, in this option, the president quietly proposes to her board of trustees that the college will name an academic building in his honor, that it will grant him an honorary degree at the next commencement, and that the college will create an annual lecture series in his name, focusing on the college role in teaching values and ethics. The president would offer these significant awards to the potential donor with the under-standing that he would drop the conditions he had earlier attached to his gift.

By taking this option, President Seger is using the recognition the college itself has to offer as a way to convince the alumnus to make his gift without any conditions attached to it. She is fully aware of the manipulative strategy in this approach but feels it is an acceptable way to achieve the college's goal. She feels confident in her ability to convince the board of trustees and the college faculty of this proposal, especially given the unparalleled reward represented by this large gift. The alumnus will become a revered figure at his Alma Mater, and the college will maintain its academic integrity.

QUESTIONS THAT MAY AID IN THE DISCUSSION OF THIS CASE STUDY

1. Should President Seger have anticipated this problem with this conservative donor before it became such a difficult issue? Over the 4 years that she met with him, couldn't she have explained what is possible and acceptable at the college?
2. How does a president keep such a sensitive issue confidential? Is this easier in a private college than in a public institution?
3. Wealthy people often have multiple interests and are frequently approached by a variety of nonprofit associations for large gifts. How much time can President Seger take with this donor before he loses his patience and decides to give his money to someone else?
4. Is President Seger endangering the academic integrity of the college by making any compromise with this potential donor?

Suggested Readings Related to This Case

Council for Advancement and Support of Education. (2009). *CASE Reporting Standards and Management Guidelines for Education Fundraising.* Washington, DC: Author.

Fischer, Marilyn. (2000). *Ethical Decision Making in fundraising.* New York: Wiley and Sons.

Kouzes, James M., & Posner, Barry Z. (2006). *A Leader's Legacy.* San Francisco: Jossey Bass.

Lansdowne, David, & Panas, Jerold. (2007). *Fundraising Realities Every Board Member Must Face.* Medfield, MA: Emerson and Church Publishers.

Chapter 2

CASE STUDIES II:
ATHLETICS AND FACILITIES

ESTABLISHING A NEW INTERCOLLEGIATE FOOTBALL
PROGRAM AT EASTERN STATE COLLEGE

A PROPOSED NEW ARENA AT GRESTON UNIVERSITY

CHANGING THE NICKNAME OF LUNDGREN
UNIVERSITY'S ATHLETIC TEAMS

ESTABLISHING A NEW INTERCOLLEGIATE FOOTBALL PROGRAM AT EASTERN STATE COLLEGE

SUMMARY OF THE CASE

Founded in 1961, Eastern State College is still a young institution. It started its modest intercollegiate sports program a few years later and now fields teams in six sports for women and six for men. There are no athletic scholarships at Eastern; its teams are often competitive, but there is only modest support for these events from students, faculty, and the local community. There is great enthusiasm for football in the state, but there has been little clamor at Eastern to establish a football program. The president of Eastern, who has earned high respect in the state and on the campus for her leadership, now wants to move the institution up academically and is seeking ways to make it more visible. Establishing a new football program is among the ideas she has to accomplish this goal.

A DESCRIPTION OF EASTERN STATE COLLEGE

Eastern State College was established by its state legislature in 1961 and is 1 of 12 state-supported public colleges and universities in its state. It is located in a city of more than 1 million people and offers a variety of undergraduate and graduate programs to a student body of almost 11,000 students. It is the youngest of the publicly supported colleges in its state and has grown steadily since its founding almost 40 years ago. Its largest academic programs are in education, health, business administration, communications, and accounting.

The president of Eastern is Rosa Francis, who has been in the position for 6 years. She is highly regarded by the faculty, students, and alumni at Eastern and is also well respected by the community and in the state legislature. A strong advocate for improved access to higher education in the state, she has earned a reputation as a passionate and persuasive champion for minorities, low-income citizens, and first-generation students. The board of trustees at Eastern consists of 12 citizens appointed by the state's governor, and the board feels it is fortunate to have Rosa Francis as its president and has worked to keep her at Eastern.

The director of intercollegiate athletics at Eastern is Frank Douglas, who reports to President Francis. Douglas has been in his position at Eastern since 2004, having been a head basketball coach for several years at a college in the Midwest before coming to Eastern. In addition to his role as director of intercollegiate athletics, he is also the head men's basketball coach at Eastern. There is a college athletics council composed of eight faculty, two staff, and two students, which oversees the intercollegiate athletic program, monitors its activities, and makes recommendations to the president.

The intercollegiate sports program at Eastern includes six teams for women (basketball, gymnastics, volleyball, lacrosse, soccer, and swimming) and six teams for men (basketball, ice hockey, lacrosse, wrestling, swimming, and track and field). There are no athletic scholarships at Eastern, no special consideration given to athletes in admissions, and no special campus services only for athletes. Students who participate in intercollegiate athletics at Eastern earn slightly higher grades than nonathletes and graduate from Eastern in four years at a rate of 68 percent, compared with 57 percent for the regular student body. Some of the coaches for the various sports also have other part-time assignments within the college, in such offices as alumni affairs, student housing, and career advising.

The sports teams at Eastern compete in an athletic conference of eight colleges with similarly defined athletic programs. Because these colleges are all located within a 5-hour driving distance, travel costs are kept to a minimum. The intercollegiate athletics program at Eastern is supported almost entirely by a required student fee and with an annual allocation from the regular institutional budget. Only the men's basketball program charges a fee to attend its games, so the income from ticket revenue is minimal. Some of the teams have local boosters' clubs, but contributions to these clubs usually amount to less than $20,000 per year for all sports. The facilities for Eastern's sports teams have been built with state funds over the years and are maintained by the institution out of its general budget.

Eastern State is often described in the press as a commuter-based institution without a clear identity or brand and as an economical, if un-exciting, place to go to college. It is "overshadowed" by three larger, and much older and more established universities in its state—two of them state supported and one private. All three of these universities have large and highly visible intercollegiate football programs and, as a result, are often in the news. Some of the students at Eastern leave their own campus on weekends to attend football games on these three campuses and to participate in the more active social life associated with the games.

THE STUDENTS AND THE FACULTY

The student body at Eastern comes almost entirely from within the state, and many of the students continue to live at home and commute to class each day to save money. Almost 65 percent of Eastern students are the first in their families to attend college, and 40 percent of the students are ethnic minorities. Most of the students who apply to Eastern are admitted, reflecting the institution's reputation for being an open, welcoming, and supportive college for students. There are extensive academic support services provided, and with the nurturing environment on campus, the graduation rate is quite high. Although there is not much "school spirit" in the traditional sense, most students enjoy their academic experience at Eastern.

There are many student clubs and organizations, although student life is not as active as on more traditional, residential campuses. Only about 800 students live in campus residence halls, and the rest either commute from home or live in apartments close to the campus. Students who participate on the intercollegiate sports teams at Eastern are enthusiastic about the experience and take pride in their sport. Although attendance is free at all events except men's basketball, it is rare to have more than a few hundred spectators for a game or meet. Students pay a required fee of $90 per semester to support the inter-collegiate and intramural sports programs at Eastern; this fee is built into their tuition, and most students are not even aware that they pay it. The campus recreation building, open to students, faculty, and staff, is one of the most popular facilities at Eastern. There are dozens of student and faculty teams in a variety of sports, and over half of Eastern students use this facility every week. The fitness program is especially popular.

More than 80 percent of Eastern students are recipients of financial aid, most of it coming from federal and state sources. The institution prides itself for keeping its costs low, and typical student costs for an academic year total less than $14,000. Almost half of the students work during the academic year, most often in the city, but many of them are employed in campus offices. Reflecting President Francis' priorities on access, Eastern works hard to support its students and discourages them to borrow too much money while in college.

The faculty at Eastern reflect the diversity in the student body and are strongly committed to teaching and service. Most of them were attracted to Eastern for its emphasis upon undergraduate education and for the opportunity to work in an evolving, urban institution with students from modest socioeconomic backgrounds. Publication and research are important, but the clear emphasis at the institution is on teaching. Most faculty teach three to four courses per semester and also spend considerable time advising students and helping them with their academic and personal concerns. In the state, Eastern has a well-deserved reputation as a caring college where students are treated in a personal manner. Most of this is due to the faculty.

In the past few years, there has been some unrest among the faculty, especially those who have been at Eastern for less than 10 years. While the college experiences modest enrollment growth each year, these faculty want it to grow more rapidly and, especially, to develop more graduate programs and research opportunities. These younger faculty would like Eastern to compete for students with better academic records and to gain more visibility within the state and the geographical region.

THE ISSUE FOR THIS CASE STUDY

President Francis is genuinely committed to open access and opportunity and has been successful at Eastern in earning support from the legislature and board of trustees. The institution has solid public support and has managed to avoid problems that might bring negative publicity to it. But President Francis does have further ambitions for Eastern and wants to move the institution forward by increasing its enrollment, making research a stronger priority in faculty hiring and promotion, improving the academic quality of the entering students, building more graduate programs, and significantly expanding the visibility of the institution in the state and region.

President Francis has several ideas that she plans to pursue over the next few years to accomplish her goals at Eastern, and among them is her desire to add football to the list of intercollegiate sports at the institution. Knowing how popular this sport is in her state and region, she is convinced that adding football would help make the institution more visible and would likely bring new supporters to the campus who could become important in helping her reach her goals. She has been the successful leader at Eastern for 6 years and feels confident that she can make this happen. But she also knows she will face many obstacles and she will need to be very persuasive in dealing with a variety of groups and individuals.

She has quietly discussed this idea of adding football with key members of her board of trustees, because she knows she cannot succeed in this idea without their support. While the board members she consulted raised many doubts about the feasibility and desirability of a new football program, their respect and admiration for President Francis led them to give her their nonpublic go-ahead. She, of course, is aware of the difficulties she will face, but she was pleased that the board members she met with did not clearly reject her idea.

President Francis also knows that she cannot create a football program at Eastern without the support and participation of the seven other colleges in the athletic conference of which Eastern is a member. However, she knows her presidential colleagues in these institutions, and she is confident that they share her goal of establishing new football programs. She has been assured by three of them that as soon as a majority of the colleges in the conference make their desire public to add football, it will become a reality. But President Francis also knows that at Eastern, there are likely to be more objections to moving in this direction due to its low-key approach to sports and, especially, to its traditional emphasis on access as the hallmark of the institution.

President Francis also knows that football, even without scholarships and highly paid coaches, will be, by far, the most expensive sport at Eastern, essentially doubling the costs in the athletic program. Without additional funds (there isn't even a campus football field or stadium), she knows she will have to find money to fund this new endeavor. Even if she can do this, she knows adding football will upset the "balance" between men's and women's sports and will likely result in some resentment and anger among the existing student athletes and coaches. Moreover, because of the legal requirements of Title IX, Eastern might have to eliminate one men's sport or add another women's sport to remain in compliance with the rules.

Students at Eastern already fund the largest portion of the athletic budget via a required fee of $90 per semester. Although there has been no objection from students to this fee, most students are not even aware of the fee because it is part of their tuition. President Francis knows that if a new football program is to be added, a significant increase in this required student fee will have to occur. At a time when many students' families are facing serious economic problems, and some have lost their jobs, the president knows this will be difficult to sell to her students. There has been no movement among students to add football during the past several years, and what little enthusiasm there is at Eastern for sports is almost entirely given to men's basketball.

The athletic director at Eastern, Frank Douglas, is also the head men's basketball coach. His basketball team has had some modest success, having won two conference championships in the last 6 years. But Douglas' decision 3 years ago to charge $5 a ticket to attend home men's basketball games has not produced significant revenue. Moreover, it is rare when more than a few hundred spectators attend a game. Douglas is the athletic director, but he is mainly a basketball coach, and President Francis suspects Douglas will not only object to adding football but would not be capable of making the football program a success because of his limited leadership experience and fundraising activities. She imagines to herself that Douglas may choose to leave his position to seek another head basketball coaching position elsewhere if a new football program is begun.

The faculty senate at Eastern has been active for several years, but its main focus has been on the undergraduate curriculum and salaries. It has had a mostly cordial relationship with President Francis and her administration, and it has been supportive of her commitment to access and opportunity at Eastern. To the best of her knowledge, members of the faculty are not aware of her interest in creating a football program, although they certainly are aware of her desire to transform the college into a university, especially her intent to upgrade the academic quality of the faculty. Because some faculty have been outspoken in their objections to upgrading the academic standing of Eastern, President Francis knows that she can expect some resistance from faculty to a proposed football program.

Eastern State College is located in a fairly large city, and although few of the city leaders and most prominent citizens are graduates of Eastern, they are supportive of the institution and want it to be an attractive asset to the city. They have good relations with President Francis, and she has been an active participant and leader in business and professional associations in the city. She is viewed by the business community of the city as an effective public advocate for the city's future. As a result of some private conversations with some local business leaders, she knows they have an interest in creating a football program at Eastern, and she is confident that she could secure their public support (and financial contributions!) for it. The business and elected leaders of the city have long been envious of three other, smaller cities in the state where the well-known and nationally competitive football programs exist at their universities. They would like to see Eastern begin its own football program, however modest it might have to be in its early years.

SOME OPTIONS FOR ADDRESSING THE ISSUE

1. President Francis should present the idea of a new football program to the Eastern State College community in a public speech, at the same time announcing that she will appoint a special task force of faculty, students, staff, alumni, and city leaders for the purpose of studying this matter and making recommendations to her in the next 5 months.

This option initiated by the president has the obvious advantage of involving a broad spectrum of people in the process and invites all members of the Eastern community to become part of the process. It also provides for a legitimate forum in which the issue can be debated and discussed, and it may convince others that President Francis has not yet made up her mind about a football program and is genuinely interested in others' ideas and views. Of course, appointing such a task force may produce skepticism and even anger among some groups, as they may feel it is merely a political ploy on the president's part to justify what they feel she has already decided.

2. After some brief consultation with the faculty senate, the student government association, the intercollegiate athletics board, city leaders, and the governing board chair, President Francis should publish and announce a comprehensive plan to establish a football program, including a way to finance it, to the full board of trustees for their approval.

By taking this strong and assertive action, President Francis is leaving no doubt that the new football program is something she intends to establish at Eastern. She knows this announcement will result in considerable debate and objection; however, she is convinced that it is a positive thing to do at her institution, and she is willing to accept the criticism from those who do not like it. Moreover, for those who may have serious problems with it, such as the current director of athletics, she is willing to accept their resignations.

3. Knowing that this is a complex issue that may upset many people, President Francis should proceed with caution. She should "float" the idea with the various campus and city groups and then invite an external team of three well-respected consultants to the campus to advise the institution about whether or how to proceed. These consultants would be free to make whatever observations and recommendations to Eastern that they felt justified. The three external consultants would be an athletic director, a football coach, and a retired college president.

This option may convince people that President Francis is openly seeking expert advice on the issue before making any decision on the football program at Eastern. There may be objections to spending money on such consultants, especially when many within the institution feel there are more important things to spend money on now than a new football program. At the same time, it may be wise to obtain such valuable advice before proceeding with such a significant new direction in the intercollegiate athletics program.

4. President Francis should trust the regular decision-making processes at Eastern and introduce the idea of a football program to various campus and community groups and invite debates and discussion on the matter for a period of several months. If there is no support for a football program, she will simply move on to another issue or delay this goal for another time.

President Francis clearly wants a football program at Eastern, because she is convinced that however small it may start out to be, it has the potential in future years to help advance the institution. However, she is not willing to risk her presidency on this one issue, especially in view of her positive image as an educational leader and an advocate of access in the state. She is not negative toward college sports and understands how important they can be to a college, but for now she would prefer to stake her future on more academic issues. This option may confirm to the campus community that President Francis is genuinely committed to wide participation and democratic decision making at Eastern. Of course, there may be skeptics in the academic community who wonder why the president may be pursuing such an idea and others who may view her as a weak leader if this process does not result in a football program.

SOME QUESTIONS RELATED TO THIS CASE

1. Should the president wait until the economic situation improves before she takes on this new football program? In view of all the other serious problems being faced by public institutions in 2010, is her timing right?
2. Can the president retain her credibility and public respect by pursuing a football program? She is well known for her support of access and academic support programs. Will others be confused by her interest in a football program?

3. Will such tactics as appointing a task force or inviting consultants to the campus be viewed as manipulation by the campus community, or will these time-honored approaches serve the president effectively?
4. Is it realistic for President Francis to raise sufficient money to support a football program? Can she convince the students to increase their required athletic fee and entice city and alumni leaders to make significant contributions to support a new football program? Will such efforts divert the president from more important goals?

Suggested Readings Related to This Case

Bowen, William G., Levine, Sarah, Shuman, James, & Campbell, Colin. (2003). *Reclaiming the Game: College Sports and Educational Values.* Princeton, NJ: Princeton University Press.

Duderstadt, James J. (2003). *Intercollegiate Athletics and the University: A University President's Perspective.* Ann Arbor, MI: University of Michigan Press. 2003.

Thelin, John R. (1996). *Games Colleges Play: Scandal and Reform in Intercollegiate Athletics.* Baltimore, MD: Johns Hopkins University Press.

Toma, J. Douglas, & Kramer, Dennis. (2010). *The Uses of Intercollegiate Athletics: Challenges and Opportunities.* San Francisco: Jossey Bass.

A PROPOSED NEW ARENA AT GRESTON UNIVERSITY

SUMMARY OF THE CASE

Greston University is a prestigious, private urban institution of 23,000 students located in a large city in the upper Midwest. Its undergraduate, graduate, and professional programs are often ranked among the top 25 in the nation. It is also well known for its successful men's and women's basketball teams, which enjoy enthusiastic support from students, staff, alumni, and the city. The basketball teams have played their games for decades in an outdated campus gymnasium, whose seating capacity is only 8,000, which makes the demand for tickets very high. Basketball fans, alumni, and students have been pushing Greston for years to build a large, new arena, and in 2009, a wealthy alumnus pledged to donate $100 million for a new arena. Greston administrators want to build the new arena on land the institution owns adjacent to the main campus, but in an area where Greston still has several buildings that contain space leased by the university to various offices, local businesses, and some individual apartments. The buildings are located in a run-down area of the city that has been plagued by crime problems for many years. Greston University is eager to place its new arena on this site, but as it makes its plans to do so, it faces vigorous opposition from some city leaders and local residents, and even from some of its own faculty, students, and alumni.

A DESCRIPTION OF GRESTON UNIVERSITY

Greston University was founded in 1885 by a group of Lutheran ministers determined to provide higher education mainly to the Scandanavian immigrants they were serving in their churches. The young institution barely managed to survive its earliest years, but by 1915, its enrollment reached 900. Thanks to some generous donors, it was able to expand its curriculum and build an attractive campus in the city. By World War II, its enrollment had grown to 8,500, the institution had severed its original ties with the church, and Greston had added schools of medicine and law. The university grew rapidly after the war, and when its enrollment reached 23,000 in 1980, its board of trustees decided to keep the enrollment at that level for the future.

Greston has 16,000 undergraduates and 7,000 graduate and professional school students. It has earned national recognition for its academic programs, and many of its graduates are well-known political, academic, business, and professional leaders. The past two governors of the state were Greston graduates, and two current U.S. senators from other states have Greston degrees.

The university maintains good relationships with the six public universities in its state but does not often compete for undergraduates with them, as Greston attracts its students from all 50 states and many foreign countries. The institution is viewed as a valuable asset by the city in which it is located, although few students at Greston grew up in the city. Elected leaders understand the prestige and visibility that Greston University adds to the city, although some of them occasionally express resentment about the academic elitism and affluence they feel Greston represents.

The university is governed by a self-perpetuating board of trustees. Its members include some nationally prominent business, professional, and political leaders and some of the leading citizens of the city. The board has tried to be socially progressive in its actions in the past 25 years, especially in view of Greston's location in a large city, and in a neighborhood with high unemployment and serious crime. Greston has a vice president for community relations, who works closely with the mayor and the city council to ensure open communications with city and university leaders.

Thanks to excellent leadership by Greston's presidents, its board of trustees, and the Greston University Foundation board, the institution has a substantial endowment, which reached almost $7 billion in 2008. During the serious economic downturn since then, the endowment has decreased in value by about 20 percent, but leaders at the university are optimistic that the endowment will return to its earlier value and continue to grow in the future. This large endowment has been important in enabling Greston to achieve national and international academic prominence.

Margaret Brown was appointed president of Greston University in 2004, having previously served as provost of a similar, high-prestige private urban university in the Northeast. She has a medical degree and previously taught in a medical school in another state before becoming a provost. She was attracted to Greston because she is convinced that a high-quality, urban private institution in one of the nation's largest cities offers tremendous opportunities to advance knowledge and prepare leaders for the future. She also knows that Greston's substantial endowment will enable the university to compete at the highest levels of academia, but she knows as well that she will have to keep pushing her institution to increase this endowment.

With such a strong emphasis on academic excellence at Greston, it is a matter of some surprise, but also great pride, that the university has enjoyed so much success over the past 25 years in its basketball programs. Most of the other sports teams at the university do not excel at this level, but students, staff, alumni, and city residents are very enthusiastic about basketball! The university does grant athletic scholarships and has been able to attract outstanding young men and women basketball players from high schools from around the country. The basketball games are often on television, and Greston feels this visibility helps to advance the university. Demand for home basketball tickets is so high that deciding who has access to them is annually a matter of considerable debate. Students, staff, alumni, and city-based fans have been eager for a larger, more modern basketball arena for years!

THE STUDENTS AND THE FACULTY

The undergraduate students at Greston University come from all 50 states and several other countries. They come mostly from affluent backgrounds, and virtually all of them have been top students in their secondary schools. Competition for admission to Greston is very high, and the admissions office is under great pressure from alumni, who would love to have their sons and daughters attend the institution. There were almost 20,000 applications for the 4,100 spaces in the latest entering freshman class.

President Margaret Brown has been successful in convincing the board of trustees to use more money from Greston's endowment to increase the diversity of the undergraduates. She does not want the institution to become an exclusive university, where first-generation students from lower income families cannot attend due to its high cost. Greston is one of a small number of highly selective institutions that have guaranteed to talented, low-income students that they can attend the university and graduate with no debt after 4 years. This was the result of President Brown's initiatives with the board of trustees. With the decrease in the endowment, the board is worried about whether Greston can continue with this policy. But it has already resulted in more economic and ethnic diversity at the university, and the president, the board, and the faculty are pleased with this outcome.

About half of Greston's undergraduates live on the campus in residence halls, and there is a demand for more on-campus housing from students and their parents, due mainly to the threat of crime in areas close to the campus and the high costs of living in the city. Academic competition among students to excel is high, and this has been a concern to the faculty and student affairs staff for some years. As a result, counseling and health services are heavily used. Students do not yet have a modern recreation center on campus, and many of them are hopeful for such a facility.

Student life at Greston is quite lively, although the students seem to spend most of their time studying during the week and then partying on weekends. Alcohol abuse among students has been a serious issue for several years, and the university has educational, prevention, and treatment programs in place for this problem. There are 240 student groups on campus, reflecting the many social, religious, political, and recreational interests of the student body. Almost half of the undergraduates are engaged in some kind of international experience during their 4 years at Greston, mostly in study abroad programs in Asia, Europe, South America, and Africa. This international emphasis has been important at Greston for many years and is reflected in the work of its faculty as well.

The student government association is the coordinating body for student groups at Greston and, with the mandatory student activity fee that it has at its disposal, allocates funds to these student groups for a variety of functions. Although Greston had several student groups active in city politics during the 1960s and 1970s, student interest in such matters now seems to have waned.

The students see the basketball teams as a fun outlet for their enthusiasm and energy and eagerly support the players and attend the games. They have devised their own complicated system of allocating the limited number of tickets they are granted to the games, based mainly on the number of academic credits students have accumulated. This means that most freshmen and sophomores may get to attend only two or three games per season due to the small seating capacity of the old campus gymnasium where the home games are played. No such attendance issue is faced by any of the other men's and women's sports at Greston.

The academic and professional aspirations of Greston students are high, and over one third of them go on to well-known graduate and professional schools after graduating from the institution. Students who attend Greston are aware of the university's national reputation and the high expectations others have for their success. Greston's students are respected for their academic excellence and also for their enthusiasm for their basketball teams!

Faculty members at Greston University are among the most distinguished in the country in their respected fields, and they represent the most diverse part of the institution. Faculty come from many foreign countries, and almost all of them are engaged in international activities. They are strongly research oriented, and annually the faculty attract external funds for their work that places Greston in the top 15 private universities in federal research support.

Obtaining a faculty position at Greston is very competitive, and earning tenure as a faculty member is even more strenuous. Faculty are well paid and have generous professional development opportunities, which the president and board of trustees understand are critical to attracting and retaining the high level of faculty on which the institution depends. Few faculty leave their Greston positions for similar roles at other institutions.

The university has seven colleges, not including the schools of law and medicine. The most popular undergraduate majors are biology, engineering, history, and economics. Greston has doctoral programs in most major academic disciplines, and its graduate programs in physics, chemistry, history, and biology are among the most respected in the nation.

Most of the faculty at Greston do not live close to the campus but in other areas of the city and its surrounding suburbs. Finding affordable and convenient housing for newly recruited faculty, especially in areas where crime is not a major issue, has been a concern of the institution for several years. Recognizing this as a potential obstacle to attracting talented new faculty to the university, the board of trustees has authorized the use of some endowment funds to provide low-interest housing loans to new faculty.

Faculty members at Greston are very busy and, of course, spend most of their time on their academic work, mainly in their own departments. Their interest in the campus-wide faculty senate is limited, and most of them pay little attention to its business except when the senate is considering an issue that may directly affect them.

Most faculty at Greston are not enthusiastic supporters of the sports teams, but some of them do attend the games, especially basketball. Some members of the faculty have been outspoken in what they view is an overemphasis on the men's and women's basketball programs, although the athletic department does not lose money, and almost all of the students on the teams graduate in 4 years. These outspoken faculty believe that the extensive television coverage of the basketball games gives the university an "athletic image" instead of an academic one, and they also believe that money spent on intercollegiate athletics could be better invested in more academic facilities and support.

THE ISSUE TO BE ADDRESSED IN THIS CASE STUDY

For many decades in the upper Midwest, interest in basketball has been intense. The sport is part of the culture, especially in high schools and in small towns. Thus, it has been considered "natural" that students, staff, alumni, and city residents would be enthusiastic supporters of Greston University's basketball teams. Basketball serves as a way to rally around a common cause at the institution, and cheering wildly at games has probably done more to relieve stress among students at Greston than anything else!

When the Greston's men's basketball team made it to the quarter finals of the national tournament in 2006, it was considered a great achievement for this institution with such high academic standards. Although the team lost in the quarter final game, considerable national publicity focused on the university, its various teams, and its academic accomplishments. Students, faculty, alumni, and friends of the university basked in this attention, and their support and enthusiasm for their basketball team were enhanced even further.

The old campus gymnasium where Greston's basketball teams have played its games for decades is almost depressing in its appearance and years out of date compared with other college basketball arenas throughout the country. The success of the Greston basketball teams inspired many supporters of the university to try to convince the institution to build a new arena. After many months of discussion, a wealthy alumnus offered to donate $100 million for a large, first-class arena at Greston! The university community was stunned with this gift and honored the donor at a huge rally in the old campus gymnasium. President Margaret Brown accepted this generous gift on behalf of the university and announced that planning would begin at once for this new addition to the institution.

The donor, a 1951 graduate of Greston, made most of his fortune in real estate and banking. He is not a resident of the city where the university is located, but he is a loyal basketball fan! He had not previously donated money to the institution, but the development staff at Greston had been meeting with him for the past 3 years, hopeful that some project would eventually capture his attention. Even the development staff was surprised with the amount of the gift, which is the third largest in the university's history.

As with other major urban universities, space for new buildings is at a premium, and in this situation, Greston does not have many realistic choices about where to build the proposed arena. In its early years as an institution, the board of trustees wisely purchased additional land adjacent to the campus and, since that time, has been able to expand the campus by constructing academic buildings and student residences on that land. Indeed, this is how Greston was able to construct the facilities for its law and medical schools more than 50 years ago. Now, in 2009, there is only one parcel of such land remaining, and six old buildings are located on it. These buildings, constructed in the early 1960s by a private developer who leased the land from the university, contain some business offices and some apartments used by low-income city residents. The site and its buildings are unattractive, and Greston administrators have previously considered ways to raze the buildings, clean up the area, and construct a new academic facility on the site. The proposed new arena seemed to present them with this opportunity.

As soon as President Brown announced the university's plan to build the new arena on the site, considerable discussion and debate on campus and in the city began. Some Greston faculty members voiced their opposition to the project, arguing that the institution should not spend such a huge amount of money on sports and that the donor should be asked to redirect his gift to academic programs. They further argued that spending so much money on a "basketball palace" would send the wrong message about the university—that it has now elevated sports to an almost professional level. Two student groups, while clearly not speaking for the entire Greston student body, voice their objection to the proposed arena, saying it would displace poor residents of the neighborhood, making the university appear like a giant corporation, destroying six half-century old buildings for its own entertainment. To the surprise of the president, some Greston alumni also expressed opposition to the project, preferring that the old campus gymnasium be refurbished and that the proposed site be used for needed academic buildings. The most serious opposition to the site for the new arena came from some elected city officials and local residents, who said the university should become a better neighbor in the city and "use its millions to improve living conditions close to its campus."

Greston University administrators have few other realistic choices in terms of a site for the proposed facility unless they were to purchase land somewhere in the city. This would be expensive and also would place the facility away from the campus. There is a professional basketball team in the city, which has its own large arena, but it is located eight miles from the campus, and Greston's use of that arena would be in continuous conflict with the professional team's schedule. Thus, President Brown has concluded that if the arena is to be built, the only real choice is the site where the old buildings are located. It is literally across the street from the campus.

The debate about the proposed site for the arena became very public when elected officials discussed it at a televised city council meeting. Several city residents of the affected neighborhood voiced their objection to the proposed project, and when Greston's vice president for community relations tried to defend it, he was met with loud and raucous opposition. The city's mayor, who also serves as chair of the city council, finally decided to adjourn the meeting after almost 2 hours of noisy demonstrations. To the dismay of Greston administrators, the proposed arena had become the center of a controversy, and the university was being portrayed by many in the press as the villain.

In the next few weeks, newspaper and television coverage about the proposed arena became quite extensive, and demonstrators picketed the proposed arena site almost daily with signs critical of the "insensitive," "power-hungry" university. At the same time, there were formal statements of support for the project expressed by the student government association and the alumni council. However, the faculty senate, after debating the matter for more than 3 weeks, voted not to endorse the proposed project.

President Brown stayed in close communication with her board of trustees during the 5 months since the controversy over the site began. She is well aware that many students, staff, alumni, and city basketball fans are anxious to see this arena get built, and she is also aware of their impatience with those who oppose it. She knows it is important to maintain good relations with the city and wants her institution to be a responsible corporate citizen. In facing this issue, President Brown and her colleagues at Greston are considering at least the following options.

SOME OPTIONS FOR ADDRESSING THIS ISSUE

1. Move ahead with the project and build the arena on the proposed site.

Greston University owns the land where the arena is to be built and has all the legal rights to the land and the old buildings located there. As an urban institution, it has to accept the inevitable criticism from various organizations, elected officials, and individual residents no matter what action it takes. Moreover, the institution is confident that once the new arena is completed, it will become a symbol of pride for the city and the university, and the current opposition being expressed to it will be mostly forgotten. President Brown is a strong administrator and is willing to take the public criticism that she will get during this lengthy process. The generous gift from the alumnus represents a golden opportunity for her university to accomplish an important goal, and she is determined to not back down in the face of the public opposition to this project. She is confident that she has the support of her board of trustees in moving ahead with the project and looks forward to the opening of the new arena.

In this option, President Brown decides to move ahead with the project after hearing months of debate and argument from many groups and individuals. She has met with city officials, neighborhood groups, and faculty, students, and alumni, and she has concluded that no consensus can be reached, because there are too many opinions and too many private agendas associated with the project and the site. The longer she allows this debate to continue, the worse the situation will get, she feels. She knows she will be criticized publicly for deciding to go ahead and build the arena on the site, but she recognizes and accepts that this is something she has to expect as the leader of her institution. As a matter of fact, she feels that the faster she can move ahead and get the arena built, the better off her institution will be.

2. Work with city officials and neighborhood groups and form a joint university–city committee to study the issue for 4 months and try to resolve it.

In this option, President Brown decides the issue is too divisive to ignore the public opposition to the use of the proposed site from elected officials and concerned residents of the neighborhood. Moreover, she is worried about the uneven support for the proposed project from within the campus itself, especially from the faculty senate. Most of all, she knows how important it is for Greston University to maintain good relationships with the city, its elected leaders, and community organizations. Thus, she approaches the mayor and other city officials, and they agree to appoint a joint committee to demonstrate the cooperation between the city and the university in solving the problem. She feels if she were to ignore those who have expressed their opposition to the project, she and the institution will be perceived as arrogant, distant, and insensitive to the very city that hosts her institution. Although she is concerned that such a joint committee might not resolve this issue and may actually intensify the opposition to the proposed arena, she sees few other good alternatives. She plans to be an active contributor to the committee and expects her vice president for community relations to persuade it to submit a recommendation to move ahead with the project. She also knows the donor who is making the new arena possible may become impatient and angry with her for what he believes is an unnecessary delay in the project. Moreover, while her own board of trustees is supportive, she knows it is also impatient and wants to rid itself of this issue.

President Brown is not optimistic about the ability of this committee to resolve this issue, as the feelings from many groups are too diverse and volatile. But she feels this strategy is a necessary step in buying some time so that some of the anger and frustration may dissipate for a while. In effect, she is hoping the committee will diffuse the issue and create a legitimate and rational forum for useful discussion and debate to occur. Whatever the actual outcome and recommendations of the committee, she feels it represents a real effort on the university's part to be a responsible corporate citizen and will discourage opponents to continue to accuse the university of not being sensitive to city residents. She and her staff will be active participants in the committee's work and will also quietly meet with elected officials and neighborhood residents to discuss the project in the coming weeks. Finally, President Brown assures the city that Greston University will not proceed with the proposed arena until the committee's report is completed and until there has been a full opportunity for everyone to comment on it.

3. Build the arena on the proposed site and include additional facilities in it that will be open to residents of the neighborhood.

President Brown has had valuable previous leadership experience in an urban university and understands how to negotiate. She also has a strong social conscience and feels her university has an obligation to serve the needs of city residents more directly, especially those within the environs of the institution. She believes that Greston should demonstrate its commitment to the city in more visible ways than it has in the past. She is determined to see the new arena become a reality and in this option decides to expand the plans for the building by adding a recreation center, a dance and music studio, and a child-care center to the facility. Most important, she will make these facilities open to res-

idents of the neighborhood. In effect, the residents of the area will have access to services provided by the university at either no cost to them or for very afford-able fees. President Brown believes this action will demonstrate to the city and neighborhood residents that the university wants them to feel they are a part of it. She is confident that this option will gain sufficient support from the city and the neighborhood that she will be able to move ahead with the arena. She knows this action will be opposed by some students and alumni, who feel that university facilities should only be open to them, but she feels making these attractive facilities open to the residents of the neighborhood is a very small "price" to pay for making it possible to build the arena. She also feels it is the right thing for the university to do as a good corporate citizen of the city.

In this option, President Brown and her staff decide to use the new arena as a way to demonstrate the university's commitment to the city and the neighborhood residents. The Greston students have wanted a recreation center for many years, and the arena is an ideal place to locate it. Moreover, its costs can be covered by a modest student fee that will be made part of regular tuition. The dance and music studio can be jointly operated by the athletic and music departments. The child-care center will be open for use by the children of student parents but primarily by children of parents who live in the immediate neighborhood. All of these added facilities will be open to residents of the neighborhood, and the hope is that the mixing of campus and community residents in them will be beneficial to everyone. President Brown decides that she will use the university's facilities and resources to benefit the community by taking this action, and she is also confident that she has the support of the board of trustees to make this investment for the benefit of the university.

4. Decide it is not worth fighting those opposed to the proposed arena site, and seek another alternative.

President Brown is facing some difficult challenges at Greston University, especially since the recession of 2008. After listening to all the opposition to the proposed arena site, she decides that it would be best to leave the site alone and look for another alternative. She thinks serious damage to the university's rep-utation and relationships with the city will be done if she continues to fight for the proposed site. Moreover, she is confident that she can maintain the interest *and support of the donor despite this setback. A 2- or 3-year delay in building a new arena can be tolerated, and during such difficult economic times it is probably not a good idea to be constructing a $100 million sports arena anyway. The only possibility of finding a site on the campus would be to tear down three old academic buildings, and even if this could be done the large arena would overwhelm the area and detract from the beauty of the campus. The president and her staff know that there is some city-owned land only a mile from the campus, where some low-income, dilapidated housing is located. It would be expensive to purchase the land, and the politics of removing the city-owned housing there could be equally difficult to the current situation she faces. But this option not to fight those opposed to the proposed site gives Greston leaders some time and removes the bad publicity the institution is getting regarding the proposed site for the arena. Brown and her staff decide the timing is not right now, and the best alternative is to back away from this issue and address it again within the next few years.*

President Brown decides that sometimes it is wiser to retreat from a nasty fight than to continue to pursue it, especially when there are other, more important financial and academic matters that need her attention. Moreover, she does not want to embroil her institution in a public battle over a sports arena at a time when so many city residents are unemployed and struggling to keep their lives in order. She feels that she can place this issue on the table, work to improve relationships with the city, and find a better time in the future to build the arena. She is well aware that this decision to back away from the controversy may cause enthusiasts for the new basketball facility to become angry with her and to accuse her of being a timid leader. She has to be quite forceful with her own board of trustees before she can convince them that this option is the best at this time, as many of them are eager to see the new arena built. She must appeal to the good sense and loyalty of the Greston students, staff, and basketball supporters by explaining to them that the university's responsibility to the city and to its neighborhood should outweigh their enthusiasm, while assuring them that the arena will someday become a reality. Although some may criticize her for not having the courage to decide to move ahead with the proposed arena on the site, as Greston's president, she feels it has taken more courage to back away from it!

QUESTIONS THAT MAY AID IN THE DISCUSSION
OF THIS CASE STUDY

1. President Brown has on her staff a vice president for community relations, whose job is to build and maintain good communications with the city. Should he have found a way to prevent this issue from becoming such a controversy and so damaging to the university? Should the president relieve him of his duties?
2. Should the university leaders have anticipated a problem with this last piece of its undeveloped property and much earlier have done something positive about it? In an urban setting, isn't it just a matter of time before such a property will become a matter of public concern?
3. President Brown feels she is well supported by her board of trustees. But is this an issue that could become so volatile that it might result in her being removed from her position? Is this issue worth it?
4. By "bargaining" with the city or entering into a joint committee review with the city, is the university giving away its authority and limiting its prerogatives for the future?

Suggested Readings Related to This Case

Gilderbloom, John I., Mullins, R.L., & Cisneros, Henry. (2005). *Promise and Betrayal: Universities and the Battle for Sustainable Urban Neighborhoods.* New York: SUNY Press. 2005.

Keohane, Nannerl O., & Chappell, Fred. (2006). *Higher Ground: Ethics and Leadership in the Modern University.* Durham, NC: Duke University Press.

Maurrasse, David J. (2001). *Beyond the Campus: How Colleges and Universities Form Partnerships With Their Communities.* New York: Taylor and Francis.

Rodin, Judith. (2007). *The University and the Urban Revival: Out of the Tower and Into the Streets.* Philadelphia: The University of Pennsylvania Press.

CHANGING THE NICKNAME OF LUNDGREN UNIVERSITY'S ATHLETIC TEAMS

SUMMARY OF THE CASE

Lundgren University is a large, public institution in the western United States. Students, faculty, alumni, and others throughout the state are enthusiastic supporters of its intercollegiate athletic teams, especially football and men's basketball. These games are frequently on television, and both teams are usually quite competitive at the national level. These sports have served as an effective way to build loyalty to the institution, especially among alumni. For almost 100 years, the athletic teams at Lundgren have had the nickname "Comanche Warriors," and there is a great deal of pride at the institution and in the state about this nickname and the symbols used to depict the "Comanche Warriors." However, a group of faculty, students, and Native Americans in the state complained that this nickname is racist, because they say it depicts the Comanche warrior as a stereotyped, violent savage. At about the same time, the National Collegiate Athletic Association (NCAA) became involved, and after reviewing the matter, the NCAA governing board gave the institution 4 years to change the nickname and its symbol. Failure to do so would prohibit Lundgren's athletic teams from competing in conference championship and postseason games and may cause some rival institutions to refuse to compete against Lundgren. The president of Lundgren is facing a great deal of pressure on this matter, and he stongly regrets that this issue has become so public, controversial, and divisive that other, more urgent financial and academic issues have been ignored.

THE INSTITUTION

Lundgren University enrolls 24,000 students and is the largest and most comprehensive public institution in its state. It was established in 1890 and includes professional schools of law, medicine, and veterinary medicine. About 20 percent of its students are enrolled in graduate programs, and the institution is the most selective university in the state. It is particularly well known for its research programs in agriculture, especially in agronomy and soil science.

As the first public university in its state, Lundgren has enjoyed good support over many decades from the state legislature. Many of its graduates are elected members of the legislature, and six governors and eight U.S. senators of the state have been Lundgren graduates. Since 1965, however, as the state's population has grown significantly and new public universities have been established, Lundgren's dominance in the state legislature has waned. It is located in a rural area of the state, away from the state's three large cities, and has to compete with the large, local legislative delegations from these cities, each of which now hosts a public university.

Franklin Russell is the president of Lundgren and has been in his position for 6 years. He was recruited to Lundgren in 2004 from another public university in the Southeast, where he had been president for 5 years. He is a botanist and is a recognized scholar and researcher in this field. However, he was hired as Lundgren's president primarily for his successful leadership as president of his previous university, especially for his ability to work cooperatively with the state legislature, for his ability to bring harmony among the institution's often combative academic units, and for his ability to raise private funds. He was also attractive to the board of trustees at Lundgren for his successful record in recruiting more minority faculty and students at his previous institution. As an African-American man who came from a poor family, he has been a strong advocate during his long academic career for minorities and first-generation students.

Lundgren University enjoys enthusiastic support from its students, alumni, and the public for its intercollegiate athletic teams. Although the institution barely breaks even financially in its overall sports program, the football and men's basketball games are well attended, and season tickets are in high demand. Home football games are a time when university supporters rally around the institution, and President Russell and his staff use these events to enhance support for the university, especially in building good will with constituents and introducing potential donors to the institution.

Reflecting the difficult economic times, Lundgren University has had to make significant cuts in its overall budget since 2008, including the elimination of some positions and six underproductive academic departments. Faculty and staff have not had a salary increase since 2008, and most are fearful that forced furloughs may become necessary soon, something that two public institutions in neighboring states have implemented in the past year. President Russell is respected in the Lundgren University community, but it has been inevitable in this financial climate that he has been the object of considerable criticism.

THE STUDENTS AND THE FACULTY

The undergraduate students at Lundgren come overwhelmingly from within the state and represent the most academically successful of the state's high school graduates. In the past 20 years, the institution has become very competitive in freshmen admissions due primarily to a rapidly expanding population, the solid academic reputation of the university, and the comparatively low costs of attendance.

Reflecting its location in a relatively small community, over half of the undergraduates live on campus, and the rest live close to the campus in private apartments. Social life at Lundgren is very active, and students are engaged in hundreds of student organizations, representing a variety of causes and interests. Most students greatly enjoy their time at Lundgren, and more than 75 percent graduate in 4 years.

The most popular academic majors for undergraduates are business administration, accounting, engineering, and biology. Last year, almost 30 percent of the graduates immediately went on to either professional or graduate schools.

Graduate students represent the fastest growing segment of the student body at Lundgren, and President Russell has the support of the governing board and the state legislature for his goal of increasing graduate enrollment to comprise one third of the student body by 2020. Graduate students have come from a much more diverse group of institutions in the past 20 years, reflecting the institution's desire to become a national and international university, especially in its research programs.

Football is the one activity at Lundgren that enjoys almost the universal enthusiasm and support of the students. They have a long history of backing the football team, and during the fall semester, most student social life revolves around the games. The students for decades have loved their "Comanche Warriors" and purchase and wear many items that bear the image of the teams' mascot.

The faculty at Lundgren are much more diverse than they were only 20 years ago, and now come from other universities from around the country and world. Many of them have been at the university for 10 years or less, and most of them enjoy their work at Lundgren and intend on remaining there.

Faculty are expected to be productive scholars in their fields, and their record of obtaining outside financial support for their research has increased substantially in the past decade. Despite the economic recession, the level of external support for research has remained fairly steady in the past 2 years.

The faculty senate at Lundgren has not been especially active in the past decade, as most faculty focus their attention on their individual colleges and departments. However, since the financial recession occurred, the faculty senate has become much more active, as faculty have lobbied the Lundgren administration for salary increases, assurances that certain programs would not be eliminated, and for a greater voice in institutional decisions that affect them. This has led to some tension between the faculty senate and President Russell, and there have been discussions within the senate about a vote of no confidence in the president. However, motions to that effect have not been ratified, and no vote has yet been taken.

THE ISSUE FOR THIS CASE STUDY

Intercollegiate sports are popular at Lundgren, and when most citizens of the state and region hear about the institution, it is most often about its football and men's basketball teams. This has been the case for many decades, and for the enthusiastic supporters of these teams, it is an emotional and cherished tradition. The long-time symbol of Lundgren's sports teams (indeed, even the logo on the official university stationery!) has been an image of the "Comanche Warrior." It is instantly recognizable by almost everyone in the state and region, and it is displayed on almost everything on the campus, from clothing and souvenirs to buildings and playing fields. Those who have attended Lundgren over the years have great pride in THEIR "Comanche Warriors"!

When President Russell assumed his leadership position at Lundgren in 2004, he, of course, was aware that the long-time nickname of the sports teams at his new institution could easily be viewed as offensive to Native Americans and others and that this might become a difficult public issue for him and his institution. He quietly discussed this matter with key governing board members, but he learned quickly that this was an issue he should avoid at all costs, due to the almost visceral feelings of alumni, students, and supporters of the nickname and Warrior symbol. He had plenty of other academic and organizational issues to address as a new president, and so he decided not to raise the issue of the sports nickname on his own. In his own mind, he knew the nickname was unacceptable to many people, but he was determined to keep this issue at a very low key and, above all, did not want such a divisive and unproductive issue to define his presidency.

In 2008, a small group of Lundgren students and faculty, some of whom were Native Americans, joined with leaders of the Comanche tribe and submitted a "list of grievances" to President Russell and the board of trustees. The two most prominent issues they addressed were the nickname "Comanche Warrior," which they argued was not only racist but highly offensive, and the popular, recognized symbol and mascot of the university, the "Warrior." When this small group's report was made available to the press, a torrent of publicity took place, and there was a flood of bitter and angry reactions from students, alumni, and even elected state leaders. When the NCAA governing board became involved in the issue about a month later, and it informed officials at Lundgren that the institution's sports teams' nickname and symbol were, indeed, "hostile and abusive" in nature, and that Lundgren had 4 years to change them, the discussion and debate became even more intense. President Russell was expected by almost everyone in the Lundgren community to react strongly to these demands to change the nickname and symbol and to stand up to the NCAA and the group that submitted its report, informing them that the institution would refuse to comply.

Lundgren University has a very small enrollment (about 200) of Native American students and only about 10 Native American faculty and staff. Other minorities comprise almost 20 percent of the student body, and President Russell and his staff pride themselves on the success the institution has had in the last 25 years not only in attracting minorities to the university but in graduating a high percentage of them. However, this success rate has not included Native American students, despite the considerable efforts of faculty and staff to assist and encourage them. The admissions staff, together with some key faculty, have reached out to Native American high school students and tribes in efforts to recruit and attract these students to Lundgren. At no time in the last 20 years have any of these staff (some of whom are Native American) reported that the name "Comanche Warrior" or the mascot symbol of the sports teams have been a barrier to attracting students. As a matter of fact, some of the Native American high school students who were contacted by the admissions staff seemed to express a degree of pride in the university's use of the nickname and symbol.

Anticipating that such as issue might become a complicated and negative problem for the university, President Russell, and two of his predecessors continued to have informal discussions with leaders of the Native American community in their state. This started in 1992. Although very little publicity was given to these discussions, the university was able to secure informal approval from these leaders that continued use of the "Comanche Warrior" nickname and symbol were not offensive to them. Such informal discussions continued yearly until the current issue became so volatile in 2008.

The student senate at Lundgren had its largest turnout ever when it decided it should take a public position on this issue. While the student senate passed a strong resolution demanding that the university refuse to comply with the NCAA mandate, there were several senators from this 50-person group who voted against the resolution, feeling that it was time for the university to become more sensitive to the feelings of others and to change this nickname and the symbol. The faculty senate of the university also took up the issue and, after some weeks of raucous debate, narrowly decided to urge President Russell not only to accept the NCAA demands but to publicly apologize to those offended by the nickname and symbol and to select new ones, acceptable to the university community. The university's athletic board unanimously voted to urge the university not to comply with the NCAA rule and to refuse to change either the nickname or the symbol. The student athletic council, comprised of 20 varsity athletes, voted to reject the NCAA motion as well, although it surprised some observers when they learned that several of the varsity athletes thought the "Comanche Warrior" nickname and symbol were, indeed, offensive and inappropriate and should be changed. Not surprising perhaps, the most adamant objection was expressed by the university's alumni council, which unanimously and angrily voted to condemn the NCAA motion and strongly urged President Russell and the board of trustees to ignore it.

When representatives of the Native American community, speaking on behalf of Comanche tribes, publicly notified the university that they now consider the nickname and mascot symbol demeaning and insulting, it added yet another significant dimension to this issue. This public statement was a change on the part of the tribes, who in past years in informal discussions with university officials had expressed no objection to the use of the nickname and mascot symbol.

Except for President Russell, it is the board of trustees that has been the object of the most attention and criticism on this issue. After being quietly counseled by President Russell and the institution's attorney, the board as a whole has been cautious, refusing to take a public position to date. Individual members have commented publicly from time to time but mostly to urge calm and civil consideration of this highly emotional issue. This has also been true of the state legislature and governor, who have mainly tried to evade this issue, as most of them do not want to antagonize their constituents, who clearly are opposed to the university "being bullied" into changing its sports teams nickname and symbol, which is the way they view the NCAA's motion.

This issue has consumed the attention of the university now for the last 6 months, and the NCAA has required a formal response from the university, due 3 months from now. President Russell strongly dislikes the unfavorable publicity this matter has brought to the institution and is concerned how it has divided Lundgren in the last 6 months. He knows he has to be the leader who somehow helps the institution resolve this matter, and he also knows this issue will define his presidency at Lundgren.

The following are some options that President Russell may consider.

SOME OPTIONS FOR ADDRESSING THIS ISSUE

1. In this first option, President Russell decides that this is a major test of his leadership, and he feels he should take direct and strong action. As a 60-year-old African American man, he has experienced discrimination during his life and knows how words can be demeaning to people. For him, this is a moral decision, and he knows in his heart that the use of the nickname and mascot symbol are offensive and wrong. Thus, President Russell consults briefly with the major constituent groups concerned with this issue, including faculty, students, alumni, the athletic council, representatives of the Native American community, and his own board of trustees, and then he publicly announces that he has decided to drop the nickname and mascot symbol at the end of the next academic year. At the same time, he urges everyone to support the university, despite their strong feelings on this issue, and to recognize the importance of showing respect for Native Americans and their heritage. He also announces the appointment of a task force, representing all of these constituent groups, to recommend a new nickname and mascot symbol for the university. He gives the task force one calendar year to make its recommendation.

By taking this forceful and direct action, President Russell has decided what he thinks is right about the issue and what is best for Lundgren University. He knows his decision will be unpopular, but he feels he should be clear about his stance on the matter and does not want to bog the institution down for years in endless and highly divisive arguments about what to do. He has important academic and financial issues that must be addressed at the university, and he does not want them obscured or dominated by nonproductive discussions about a nickname! He knows he will likely be viewed by his opponents on this issue as a "nonloyal" autocrat, but he feels this is the right thing to do and that it will allow the university to move on once the decision has been made. He is also aware that this issue is volatile enough that it could result in his being dismissed from his position as president of Lundgren University. In his own mind, he has decided that if this is the result of his action, then he is willing to accept it.

2. President Russell is a wise and experienced administrator, and he knows how strongly the various constituent groups feel about this issue. He does not want this matter to focus national attention on the institution, and he feels it is such an emotional issue that it would be best for the university to challenge the authority of the NCAA to dictate policy to his institution. He knows this legal process of challenging the NCAA's mandate will be public, lengthy, and expensive. But he also knows that the mere fact of the institution filing a legal challenge will buy perhaps 3 or 4 years of time and also give the various constituent groups some time to cool down and rethink their objections. He has little confidence that the legal action will result in a court decision favorable to the university, but he knows that once a court has made a final decision on this matter, the institution will have no choice but to choose a new nickname and mascot symbol.

By taking this action, President Russell is indirectly joining with the alumni, the students, and the other groups that are adamantly demanding that the university refuse to comply with the NCAA motion. While he has carefully avoided stating his own views on the issue, he is, in effect, allowing his institution to challenge the authority of the NCAA, anticipating that the legal action will not produce the result hoped for by opponents of the motion. In this option, President Russell is hoping to buy some time and feels that an eventual court order mandating the university to accept the NCAA motion is preferable to what he considers the impossible task of gaining some resolution of the matter within the institution.

3. President Russell knows this is such a volatile issue that it just cannot be resolved within the institution without tearing the university apart, while losing needed support of alumni and other groups. The nickname and mascot are both almost sacred symbols for those who love the university. Thus, in this option, President Russell decides to retain the nickname and mascot while openly accepting the consequences of the NCAA sanction. The university's athletic teams will not be able to participate in conference championships or in post-season bowl games and playoffs. This decision is likely to disappoint supporters of the athletic teams and, especially, the student athletes. President Russell is hopeful that this will enable the university to continue with its traditions but by paying a price that in a few years may be viewed as sufficiently unattractive that an acceptable compromise may be developed.

This option enables the university to retain its sports teams' nickname and athletic mascot. Of course, it significantly removes the teams from important competition and may result in unfavorable publicity for the institution, branding it as recalcitrant and insensitive to minority groups. It could also result in a decision by some other universities to refuse to compete any longer in games with Lundgren. But in this option, President Russell feels it is necessary to retain the nickname and mascot in order to keep the peace at the institution, while remaining hopeful that eventually opponents to any change will accept a change and move on to some other issue.

4. President Russell believes and has confidence in his university's internal decision-making processes and feels this issue presents a challenge to faculty, students, staff, athletics, alumni, and the governing board to assume responsibility for tackling the issue and coming up with an acceptable decision that will be best for Lundgren University. He also feels that all of the constituent groups want to have a role in the decision-making process, and that without their direct participation in the issue, no decision can be sustained or supported. In this option, he appoints a task force, chaired by a beloved and respected former president of the university, and consisting of representatives of all the constituent groups. The assignment to the task force will be to discuss and debate the issue and, within 6 months, to recommend a solution to him and the board of trustees. President Russell admonishes the task force to "recommend a solution that will resolve the issue and serve the best interests of the university."

By taking this action to appoint a high-level task force, President Russell is affirming his confidence in the collegiate model of institutional governance and inviting the various constituent groups into the process. He is confident that such a group, representing the most respected leaders in the university community, can rationally and fairly consider this volatile issue and suggest a resolution that will be acceptable to most everyone while affirming to the public that Lundgren is a place where the feelings of all groups are respected and honored. He also knows, however, that this issue is so volatile that the task force may not be able to resolve it in a satisfactory manner and that the matter will be back on his desk, more complicated than ever.

QUESTIONS THAT MAY AID IN THE DISCUSSION OF THIS CASE STUDY

1. Should President Russell involve key members of the state legislature more directly in this issue? As a public university, can he avoid doing this? What if any role should the president ask the legislature to assume?
2. Is there an opportunity to educate the Lundgren University community about Native American history and culture in this situation? Could this result in any change in attitudes regarding the demeaning nickname and symbol?
3. Can President Russell survive this highly public issue? Should he take Option 1, feeling it is the right thing to do, and then offer his resignation to the board of trustees, assuming that this issue will so divide the institution that it will require a new leader in a year?
4. What other administrative leaders at Lundgren, if any, should have a significant role in this issue? Does the president have any choice except to be the key figure in the dispute? Should the president permit the athletic director and the coaches to speak freely in public, expressing their own views on this matter?
5. Should President Russell have considered another option—to invite a panel of outside experts to the campus to review the matter and make recommendations to him?

Suggested Readings Related to This Case

Deutsch, Morton, Coleman, Peter T., & Marcus, Eric. (2006). *The Handbook of Conflict Resolution: Theory and Practice.* San Francisco: Jossey Bass. 2006.

Kerr, Clark. (2001). *The Uses of the University* (5th edition). Cambridge, MA: Harvard University Press.

Padilla, Arthur. (2005). *Portraits in Leadership: Six Extraordinary Presidents.* Washington, DC: American Council on Education.

Wertz, Jay. (2008). *The Native American Experience.* Guildford, CT: Globe Pequot Press. 2008

Chapter 3

CASE STUDIES III:
ACADEMIC POLICIES AND ISSUES

REVISITING GENERAL EDUCATION AT WELCH STATE
UNIVERSITY

AN OPEN RECORDS LAW AND THE HIRING OF A
PROVOST

A GRADUATION ISSUE AT DEJONG UNIVERSITY

A PROPOSED NEW HONORS PROGRAM AT WERNER
STATE UNIVERSITY

A FREE SPEECH INCIDENT AT JURNIGAN STATE
UNIVERSITY

A PROPOSED BACHELOR'S DEGREE AT DAKER
COMMUNITY COLLEGE

REVISITING GENERAL EDUCATION AT WELCH STATE UNIVERSITY

SUMMARY OF THE CASE

Welch State University is a large, comprehensive institution in the western United States. It offers an extensive array of undergraduate and graduate programs, and in 2010 its enrollment is 32,000. There are 12 colleges at Welch State, not including the medical school. The new provost at Welch State is dismayed at what she views as the lack of coherence in undergraduate education at the institution and the almost complete dissolution of general education requirements for all students. She feels this situation has resulted in overly specialized undergraduate degrees and a decrease in the overall quality of the bachelor's degree at Welch State. Wanting all undergraduates at her institution to share some common intellectual experiences via the curriculum, she is determined to develop a new set of general education requirements at the university. In pursuing this goal, she knows she will need to be persuasive with her deans and the faculty.

A DESCRIPTION OF WELCH STATE UNIVERSITY

Welch State University is a public, land-grant institution located in a town of 35,000 and was established in 1915. As the population of its state grew, so did the university, which is now the largest institution in the state. After World War II, Welch State's enrollment grew rapidly, and by 1965 it had extensive graduate programs and a medical school. The university is likely to keep growing, as the state's population is still increasing, and there is strong demand for its academic programs. In 2010, the enrollment is 32,000, of which 24,000 are undergraduates.

Welch State University has a solid academic reputation and is a popular institution in its region for undergraduates due, in no small part, to its highly visible intercollegiate athletic programs. Even though it is still a relatively young university, there is enthusiastic loyalty to it among its alumni and students. As the institution and the state have grown, there are now many more applicants for the entering freshman class, and, as a result, the academic qualifications of the students have increased substantially.

The university works hard to establish positive relationships with the state legislature and the governor, and over the years it has enjoyed good support. Tuition has remained below the national average for state universities, making Welch State financially attractive to prospective students. The recession of 2008 has been difficult for the state and for Welch State. Unless state revenues increase in 2011, it is likely that some academic programs may have to be eliminated and tuition increased substantially. Since 1965, when Welch State's enrollment was 12,000, Lowell Johnson, its visionary president at the time, established the Welch State University Foundation and began a successful development program. Now, some 40 years later, the university has an endowment of almost $1 billion.

Welch State University has earned academic distinction for its graduate programs in agricultural economics, statistics, biology, and agronomy. As a result, it has been able to attract graduate students from many states and several foreign countries. The university has aspirations of someday being considered among the nation's top 25 public research universities. It enjoys enthusiastic support from its undergraduates, but it understands that its academic reputation largely rests on the quality of its graduate and research programs. The institution has been quite successful since 1990 in attracting outstanding faculty, but since the recession of 2008, it has had to cut back substantially on new faculty hiring.

The president of Welch State University is William Hardesty, MD, who has been in his position for 4 years. Before coming to Welch State, he had been dean of the medical school and vice president for health affairs at a large state university in the Midwest. President Hardesty hired Amanda Downing as the new provost of Welch State in 2010, after the provost left to accept a president's position at another institution. Provost Downing is a biologist who had served as the dean of the college of arts and sciences at another large state university in the

Southeast. With the exception of the medical school, which is located 120 miles away in a large city, the deans of the 12 colleges at Welch State all report to the provost. Because President Hardesty is frequently involved with the medical school and the research hospital, and because he is active with the state legislature and fundraising activities, provost Downing, in effect, is the senior internal administrative leader at Welch State University.

THE STUDENTS AND THE FACULTY

The undergraduate students at Welch State University come almost entirely from within the state. There are more than four applicants for each place in the entering class at the university, and so the university is more selective in the students it admits than it was only 20 years ago, when most students who applied were admitted. As costs of going to out-of-state colleges have increased, the number of high school graduates from within the state choosing Welch State as their first choice institution has increased dramatically. As the institution has become more selective, its academic reputation has been enhanced. It is now by far the most preferred public university in the state for undergraduate students. Minority enrollment at Welch State is almost 25 percent, reflecting quite accurately the diversity of the state.

The undergraduates seem to love Welch State, and few of them leave the university for other institutions. Almost 70 percent of the students graduate in 4 years, and most of the others remain until they earn their degrees from Welch State. About 20 percent of the students go on for further education, and the university expects this to increase due to limited job opportunities caused by the recession of 2008.

Campus student life at Welch State is focused mainly on social activities, intercollegiate athletics, and recreation. Only about 40 percent of the students live on campus, but the others live close to the campus in private apartments, so the university is clearly the center of their lives while at Welch State. Students are not much engaged in political or social action activities. There is concern among faculty, administrators, and townspeople about what they consider the excessive drinking and partying among the undergraduates, much of which takes place around football game weekends. Welch State administrators are embarrassed when almost annually, a national student publication lists the institution as among the "leading party schools."

Students have established their own student government association, and for many years, the president of this association is a regular member of the Welch State University board of trustees. Since the late 1960s, students have been invited to become members of most university committees and councils and have responded reasonably well to such opportunities. There are more than 400 student organizations at Welch State, and students in these groups seem more interested in their own activities than they do in debating academic or administrative policies at the institution.

Graduate students at Welch State come from a much wider background than the undergraduates, and most of them are attracted to the institution because of the reputation of specific academic programs. Most graduate students enjoy their time at Welch State but are focused almost entirely on their work in their academic departments. Almost 30 percent of the doctoral students at the university are from foreign countries, contributing to the international aspect of the institution.

The faculty at Welch State University have undergone some significant changes in the past 20 years. Due to the university's growth, and especially the expansion of its graduate and research programs, faculty hired since about 1990 have more impressive academic backgrounds than their predecessors and mainly a stronger expectation to do research. There is some tension between the older and the newer faculty about academic priorities, teaching loads, and salaries. Some of the faculty who have been at Welch State for more than 20 years believe the institution is moving away from undergraduates and from teaching while focusing too much of its resources on graduate and research programs.

Faculty are, of course, mostly engaged in their own teaching and research and are not particularly involved with governance issues, especially at the institution-wide level. There is a Welch State University faculty senate, with elected representatives from each of the 12 colleges, but it has not been very active over the years. However, since the recession of 2008 occurred, and the future of some academic programs and static faculty salaries became issues, the faculty senate has begun regular monthly meetings, in which some fairly intense debates have taken place. Most faculty continue to be involved primarily with their own academic departments and secondarily with their college at Welch State.

Faculty, especially those hired since the 1990s, have enjoyed fairly modest teaching loads and quite generous support for their research. Moreover, the centralized research office at Welch State, established in 1992, has been helpful to faculty in their efforts to compete for external funding for their research. Welch State's faculty attracted more than $80 million in external research funding in 2008 and hopes this figure will continue to increase despite the economic issues the country is facing.

There are some bad feelings among the faculty about the differences between the salaries of those in law, engineering, and the physical sciences and those in the humanities, education, and the social sciences. This has made collaboration among the faculty across college lines more difficult at times. But the institution enjoys a positive reputation among the public for its tradition of good teaching, and faculty in all the colleges continue to take their teaching responsibilities with undergraduates quite seriously. Moreover, there are rarely any substantial complaints from the undergraduates about teaching or the content of their academic programs.

THE ISSUE TO BE ADDRESSED IN THIS CASE STUDY

Provost Downing was hired as the senior academic officer at Welch State University 4 months ago, and the institution felt fortunate to attract her to this position, as she has had a highly successful career as a professor, researcher, and dean. After a thorough search process, during which she met with each of the college deans and several faculty groups, she emerged as the unanimous choice of the committee, and President Hardesty offered her the position. During the search process, Downing expressed her commitment to a collegiate style of academic governance, support for research, and, especially, increased attention to undergraduate education. She also criticized undergraduate education programs in large, research-based institutions, arguing that they have become too fragmented and specialized.

After she had been provost at Welch State University for 4 months and had conversed with college deans, faculty, students, and others, she informed President Hardesty that one of her first and most important initiatives as provost would be to transform the general education program at the institution. President Hardesty, although not surprised to hear this, asked his new provost if she really thought she could accomplish much in this area, given the power and virtual curricular autonomy each of the colleges now has. He understood exactly what Provost Downing was talking about when she argued that "Welch State students now graduate with almost no common intellectual experiences and it is possible for some students to earn degrees without taking a single course in mathematics, history, or a foreign language." The president also knew that his new provost, who had just completed a 6-year stint as an academic dean at another research university, understood that institution-wide general education programs were viewed with disdain by many faculty and as largely unnecessary by each of the colleges. However difficult the challenge, the president assured his new provost that he would not interfere in her effort, and he wished her the best of luck!

Provost Downing was not surprised to learn that the long-time institution-wide general education requirements began a process of serious erosion in the 1980s. Prior to about 1985, undergraduates had to take 30 semester credits in the "five core academic program: literature, mathematics, social science, physical science, and foreign languages before they could graduate." These general education courses were never popular with students, and many faculty did not like teaching them, because they all were basic, introductory courses. Responding to the ever-increasing demands from students (and often their faculty!) to enroll in classes they viewed as "directly relating to my career goals," the faculty introduced much more flexibility into the general education program, mainly by allowing students to meet these academic requirements by selecting from a long list of "distribution" courses related to each of the five areas. Over the next 15 years, this list of distribution requirements had become so inclusive that, in fact, the "general education program" no longer had any academic integrity to it, and students could "satisfy" their requirements by taking almost any classes they wished. After considerable debate in the faculty senate for some years, most faculty acceded to the growing power and autonomy of each of the colleges to decide on their own academic requirements for graduation. While the university still publicly listed the continuing existence of its general education program, the faculty, deans, and president all knew it was dead. Undergraduate students, turning over every 4 years, were not even aware that this major change had occurred at their institution, and most had never heard of the "five core academic program" that used to be so prominent at Welch State.

Provost Downing is keenly aware of other serious academic and financial problems facing her new university. She knows that creating a new general education program will not only be difficult, but will cause some to question her judgment about what is most important for Welch State in 2010. But she wanted to become a provost because she has strong beliefs and values about what undergraduates should learn, and she is very concerned about how poorly educated so many college graduates are in 2010. She feels that all college graduates should be conversant in core academic disciplines in order to be useful, contributing citizens. She decries what she feels is the overspecialization in undergraduate education and feels that universities have an obligation to society to produce well-rounded graduates. Thus, she decides that she will begin the process of trying to create an outstanding general education program at Welch State University and relishes the challenge!

Here are some options that provost Downing may consider.

SOME OPTIONS FOR ADDRESSING THIS ISSUE

1. Provost Downing is an experienced academic administrator and a respected scholar. After more than two decades in higher education, she understands how difficult it is to make curricular changes in undergraduate academic programs. However, she also knows how to identify problems in these programs and has strong ideas about what all undergraduates should learn regardless of their academic majors. She has been outspoken on issues of general education for the last 5 years and has authored a book on the subject, in which she was critical of the fragmentation of undergraduate education, especially at large universities. In the book, she also made substantive suggestions about what should be done to improve what students learn. Thus, in this option, Provost Downing decides to use her considerable knowledge and experience regarding general education and to present three models of a new general education program to her deans and faculty. She does this by sharing a 25-page "white paper" she has written and by describing it to the deans and faculty in a specially called faculty convocation. She vividly describes the problems and shortcomings in Welch State University's general education program and gives examples of how the institution is shortchanging its undergraduates by allowing them to concentrate their studies in just one area. She clearly indicates that she intends to see the university revise and improve its undergraduate education and offers three models that she asks the deans and faculty to consider in the coming months. She makes her "white paper" available online and distributes a copy to all members of the faculty.

In this option, the provost is letting the deans and faculty know that they have a new academic leader on campus! She is able and willing to take on difficult tasks, and she has the courage to take the lead herself on this complex issue. By presenting a very thoughtful and substantive "white paper" on the issue, she affirms that she is an accomplished and experienced scholar and is willing and capable of engaging her deans and faculty on this issue. She knows there is risk in taking such aggressive action, especially after being at Welch State as provost for only 4 months. She also knows that faculty are expert on finding ways to delay such proposals if they object to them. Finally, she knows that she has a good deal at stake as the new provost—if she fails in her effort to establish a new general education program, she may find it difficult to work with her deans and the faculty in achieving other reforms in the future.

2. Although Provost Downing is a recognized scholar on the topic of undergraduate education, she knows that some objective, outside experts on the topic could lend credibility to the process. Thus, in this option, the provost decides to confer with her college deans and invite three nationally recognized academic leaders and scholars to the campus to share their views about undergraduate education and about how other, similar universities are addressing the problem of overspecialization. Those invited are a retired provost from a large, research university, a scholar who has written extensively on general education programs and has taught such courses for many years, and a retired president of a large university in the Midwest. This three-person team will be on campus for 1 week and will confer with deans and faculty, present their own views at a faculty convocation, and meet with undergraduate students as well. They will be expected to present a written report back to Provost Downing within the 6 weeks, in which they will share their observations about Welch State's undergraduate programs and offer suggestions about how to revive and strengthen its general education program.

Provost Downing feels that this action will demonstrate to her deans and faculty that she not only is serious about her intent to address the shortcomings in the general education program, but that she is also going to pursue the matter in an orderly and scholarly fashion. By inviting highly respected experts on the issue to the campus, she can take advantage of their objective observations in her plan to create a new general education program. She expects the report that the outside experts will submit to be quite critical of what Welch State is doing in its various undergraduate programs. Although she knows this will not reflect positively on the university, she feels the report will provide her with another needed argument in persuading the deans and faculty that changes have to be made. She also knows that faculty are often skeptical of outsiders who may pretend to know more than the faculty do about their own institution. But when the report is made available to the public, she also knows that the criticisms and problems identified by the visiting group will be hard to dismiss.

3. Provost Downing is committed to a collegial form of governance. Although she is sometimes frustrated with the slow pace of change, she feels the only effective way to create and sustain an outstanding general education program is to involve the faculty directly in the process. Thus, in this option, the provost, after 2 months of thoughtful consultation with her deans and key faculty members in each of the colleges, decides to appoint a campus-wide task force, to be called "The future of undergraduate education at Welch State University." This 18-member group will consist of one faculty member from each of the colleges, two students, and two prominent alumni of the institution. Its charge from the provost will be to examine and evaluate the content of the various undergraduate curricula and to make specific suggestions on how the university can bring academic coherence and common intellectual experiences into its undergraduate programs. The task force, appointed in the fall of 2010, will be expected to submit its final report to the provost by August 2011. The provost assures the task force it will receive adequate resources to accomplish its work, and she urges the task force to engage members of the academic community at Welch State University in its activities.

By appointing this campus-wide task force, the provost is expressing confidence in the Welch State University tradition of participatory governance. She also knows that such a process, however tentative and lengthy it may be, is necessary for anything substantive to be accomplished in improving undergraduate education at her university. Although she has given the task force full freedom to address the issue, she knows she will need to meet with the group fairly often, push them to meet the deadline she has set, and urge them to be bold with their suggestions. She believes in the collegial model of governance but knows from experience that this entire process may result in no substantive changes in the general education program. She knows she must be patient in this process and publicly express her appreciation to the task force for the important work it is doing for the university. Finally, she knows that most faculty are passionately devoted to their own academic disciplines and are protective of their authority to decide what the curriculum should be in their own college. She wonders whether the faculty is willing or capable of looking beyond their own academic interests to focus on what all students should learn.

4. Having served several years as a professor and college dean, the provost is no stranger to the strong feelings of faculty regarding their own academic prerogatives and their own academic disciplines. She is aware that many faculty have disdain for teaching introductory courses, and that many of them feel it is intellectually dishonest or naïve in 2010 to establish a general education program given the vast and expanding nature of knowledge. Many faculty, she knows, are skeptical about the "benefits" of general education and view such courses as unnecessary distractions from a serious academic program. Given these realities, the provost is nevertheless determined to proceed and decides her best option is to direct her 12 college deans to work with her in developing and implementing a new general education program. The deans all report to her and are responsible for carrying out her policies. She knows the college deans are capable of changing the undergraduate academic requirements in their colleges and have adequate flexibility to include campus-wide general education courses in their curricula. Although she knows this will be difficult for the deans, she does not think the greatly increased autonomy the colleges at Welch State now enjoy is good for the university, and she is determined to get the deans to work together for common goals—not to compete with each other, as they have been doing for years. The general education program is a good opportunity for her to get the deans to think and work as a team, and she is convinced that it is the college deans that are the key to success in creating and implementing a successful general education program at Welch State University.

By selecting this option, Provost Downing has put the pressure for reform on the people who work directly for her! Although some of them may not like this option and may disagree with the entire general education idea, they are obligated to support this directive from the provost. This action on the part of the provost represents a significant change from what the deans have been used to for the past several years, when they were given almost free reign over their college affairs, especially the curriculum. Provost Downing likes the deans and is committed to building even stronger colleges at Welch State, but she refuses to allow each of the college deans to move in their own, self-serving directions with almost no regard for the interests of the larger institution. She knows she may be setting herself up for accusations from some faculty that "the new provost is an autocrat," but she is fully capable of handling such criticism.

QUESTIONS THAT MAY AID IN THE DISCUSSION OF THIS CASE STUDY

1. If Provost Downing is successful in establishing and implementing a new general education program at Welch State, what faculty should be assigned to teach the courses? Will such faculty be rewarded in similar ways as their counterparts who only teach more advanced courses?
2. What role, if any, should President Hardesty assume in this process? Should he make his views known to the academic community on

the viability of a new general education program? If the new provost asks for his direct intervention in this process, is she revealing her own weakness as a leader?

3. Many undergraduate students in 2010 are restless; they are strongly interested in taking more courses directly related to their career goals and to ones they feel will increase their chances of gaining admission to professional and graduate schools. Some of them may not react positively to new academic requirements that seem "irrelevant" to their current academic interests and goals. To what extent, if any, should the provost take into account such student views?

4. Is Provost Downing selecting the "wrong" issue to address as her first major initiative as provost at Welch State? Would it be better for her to gain some "small wins" in her first 2 or 3 years before she takes on such a complex and controversial issue as the creation of a new general education program?

Suggested Readings Related to This Case

Allen, Mary J. (2006). *Assessing General Education Programs.* San Francisco: Jossey Bass. 2006.

Jones, Elizabeth (Ed.). (n.d.). *The Journal of General Education.* State College, PA: Penn State University Press. (Yearly publication).

Ratliff, James L., Johnson, D. Kent, & Gaff, Jerry G. (2004). *Changing General Education Curriculum: New Directions for Higher Education.* San Francisco: Jossey Bass.

Zemsky, Robert. (2009). *Making Reform Work: The Case for Transforming American Higher Education.* New Brunswick, NJ:. Rutgers University Press.

AN OPEN RECORDS LAW AND THE
HIRING OF A PROVOST

SUMMARY OF THE CASE

Pendel University is a public, land-grant institution of 24,000 students located in the Midwest. It was founded in 1880 and is a comprehensive university with an excellent academic reputation and extensive graduate and research programs. The provost at Pendel is the senior academic officer of the university and is responsible for most of the internal administration of the institution. After the current provost left Pendel to assume the presidency of another university, the president appointed a campus-wide search committee to identify, recruit, and recommend candidates for the provost's position. The president intends to attract a nationally prominent educator as provost at Pendel. During the search process, it becomes evident that the strong open records law in the state presents a significant barrier to some excellent candidates, who are not willing to make their interest in the position made public for fear of jeopardizing their current status at their home institutions. This situation results in an applicant pool that does not meet the president's expectations for quality, which causes her to cancel the search. Now the president has to begin again and must decide how to proceed in her effort to hire an outstanding provost.

A DESCRIPTION OF PENDEL UNIVERSITY

Pendel University is a highly regarded public, land-grant institution located in an attractive Midwestern city of 120,000 people. Most of the undergraduates come from within the state, but the extensive graduate programs attract students from around the country and from 40 foreign countries.

The university consists of 12 colleges, the largest of which are agriculture, engineering, and arts and sciences. The only professional school at Pendel is veterinary medicine. The deans of the colleges report directly to the provost. Although there are vice presidents for finance, development, legal affairs, and student affairs, the provost at Pendel is the senior internal administrator and is responsible for most of the institution's budget. The past three provosts at Pendel have all gone on to become presidents of other state universities, after serving in their provost positions for an average of 5 years.

The state legislature has been quite supportive of Pendel University in past years, although Pendel's main competitor, another large university in its state, has usually been funded more generously probably because it includes the state's only medical school and the leading law school in the state. Since the major recession began in 2008, Pendel has been forced to reduce some of its staff, cut some nonacademic programs, and cease granting salary increases.

The president of Pendel is Patricia Glenn, an electrical engineer who has been in her position for 6 years. Previous to coming to Pendel as president, she had been a dean of engineering and then provost for several years at another public, land-grant university. She has developed mostly positive relations with the state legislature but is frustrated with what she considers the state's outdated tax structure, resulting in insufficient funds to support public higher education. She has been a vigorous advocate for additional funding for higher education and has been very active in private fundraising for Pendel. As a result, she is frequently away from the campus and has delegated much of the internal decision making to the provost.

THE STUDENTS AND THE FACULTY

The undergraduate students at Pendel come primarily from within the state. Because the state's population has not increased in the past 10 years, President Glenn has successfully lobbied the state legislature for permission to recruit more out-of-state undergraduates. This has enabled Pendel to maintain its current enrollment at 24,000, where it has stayed for several years. The institution received 8,000 applications for the 4,000 spaces in its entering freshmen class last year, so competition to gain admission is modest. Nevertheless, the students have good high school academic records, and their SAT scores are well above the national average. For undergraduates, Pendel is viewed as a solid and dependable place to earn a degree, especially in engineering and agriculture. Many of Pendel's graduates have excelled in these fields and have become generous donors to the university.

More than half of the students live off campus, but there is a lively on-campus life, consisting of some 450 student organizations and almost universal participation in informal recreational sports. Pendel's athletic programs are extensive, and students are enthusiastic supporters of the various teams.

Although there is an active student government association at Pendel, in recent years, it has showed little interest in the academic affairs of the institution, focusing most of its attention and resources on its own programs and activities. Many student groups are quite active in community service programs, which has become a matter of considerable pride to everyone at the university.

The graduate students at Pendel come from colleges and universities throughout the nation, and some 1,200 of the 4,500 graduate students come from foreign countries. The outstanding graduate programs in engineering, agriculture, and the biological sciences attract excellent students and enroll more than half of all the graduate students at Pendel.

Graduate students have expressed serious concern with inadequate funding for research and teaching assistantships during the past 2 years and, as a result, have formed a graduate student union to present their grievances to the graduate dean and the provost. Although they have found sympathy and understanding, they have been frustrated with the lack of funds to support their education. President Glenn is keenly aware of this situation, knowing that such support for graduate students is essential in attracting outstanding graduate students to Pendel and in maintaining its enrollment.

The faculty at Pendel is in transition, as the younger faculty hired since 1995 are more research oriented than the older faculty, most of whom will be retired by 2015. There has been some tension among these groups, as some of the older faculty, proud of their commitment to teaching, feel that Pendel is becoming so research oriented that it no longer gives adequate recognition to teaching, and, thus, the education of undergraduates is not viewed as a priority. The younger faculty, for the most part, pay little attention to this, as they are focused primarily on their own work and accept the fact that they will be advanced professionally in relation to their ability to secure grant money to support their research.

Faculty have largely left the administration of the university to the president and provost, and when they do participate in some form of governance, it is with their individual college and department. They have enjoyed considerable autonomy over the years and only get involved in institution-wide affairs when they feel their own concerns are affected. The 2008 economic recession has resulted in a hiring freeze and no salary increases for the past 2 years. They regret the cutbacks in support staff personnel that have occurred at Pendel, but to date they are relieved that no faculty members have been laid off.

THE ISSUE FOR THIS CASE STUDY

The state in which Pendel University is located has a strong open records law, which has been in effect for almost 20 years. It was passed by the state legislature primarily in response to continuing problems with elected officials in various city governments. These officials at times conducted their business and made decisions affecting local residents without permitting full public discussion of the issues involved. The resulting lack of trust from the public, and especially the aggressive advocacy of the states' newspapers and television stations, resulted in the legislature passing an open records law that required "the public's business to be conducted in the public." Some years later, a presidential search at one of the state's universities was targeted by the media, and a group of reporters insisted that they had a right under the open meetings law to see a list of the candidates for the position and to be present at meetings of the institution's search committee when interviews with the candidates took place and where discussions of their qualifications were discussed. Moreover, the reporters argued that they were protecting the public's right to know how their tax dollars were being used in appointing such an important public leader. This was the first time in this state when the media attempted to apply the open records law to the hiring process for administrators at a university. After weeks of heated debate, the affected institution decided to challenge the application of the open records law to its deliberations but was soundly defeated in the state's supreme court. Thus, in the mid-1990s, the open records law did, in fact, apply to public university searches.

The six public universities in the state had argued that the open records law was never intended to apply to the search process for university presidents and that such an application would result in the inability of institutions to attract the best candidates for the position. Major administrative leaders at other universities would not be willing to announce their candidacy for a president's position on another campus for fear of eroding their influence on their current campus. Moreover, some candidates did not want to face the embarrassment of being publicly rejected for a president's position. However, these arguments proved to be unpersuasive in court, and the universities and their governing boards were now subject to the open records law for their presidential searches.

President Glenn was the second president of Pendel University hired under the open records law. Although the board of trustees at Pendel was concerned about its ability to attract candidates for the position who were willing to have themselves publicly scrutinized, they were nevertheless successful in recruiting and hiring two presidents in 1998 and 2004. The board still feels some excellent candidates do not allow their names to be considered for president's positions, however, because of the state's open records law.

Although the press continued to be active in presidential searches, it had expressed almost no interest in searches for key faculty, academic deans, vice presidents, or provosts. President Glenn and her colleagues at the other state universities were pleased with this lack of attention from the press and for several years proceeded with searches for these positions without having to worry about demands from the press to participate in the process. President Glenn noted with wry humor that apparently "the public interest" was not much affected by the hiring of other academic leaders! Candidates for key faculty, academic dean, and vice presidential positions were formally notified of the public records law in the state but were also assured that, for many years, no "interference" in their hiring processes had occurred for these positions.

This situation changed in 2009 when Pendel conducted its search for its new provost. Reporters from three newspapers attended the initial meeting of the search committee and notified the chair of the committee that they would be requesting the names of all candidates and intended to cover and report on the deliberations of the entire search process. In its public advertisements for the provost's position, Pendel included the required notification that it was in an "opening records" state but, based on its past experience with such nonpresidential searches, did not anticipate that this would be a problem. Indeed, when the chair of the search committee for the provost was called on the phone by prospective candidates, the committee chair informed them that the open records law had never posed any problem because the press apparently was not much concerned about it.

When the media's interest in the search process for the public became well known, the committee chair received several phone calls from academic leaders at other institutions, informing him that, as a result of the application of the open records law to the search, they had decided not to apply for the provost's position at Pendel. The committee noted with chagrin in the next few weeks that the number and quality of the applicants did not match its expectations for quality. Of course, because the search committee discussions were public and reported in the press, the committee did not publicly reveal its true feelings about its disappointment with the lack of outstanding candidates in the applicant pool. After a private discussion with the president, the search committee chair decided to continue with the search while extending the timeline by a full month. The committee then invited four candidates to the campus for formal interviews and, after a period of 5 weeks, concluded these interviews, all of which were carefully covered by the press. Reaction from the faculty, deans, and the committee were not very enthusiastic about any of the four visiting candidates, and after careful consideration, but only guarded and muted discussion in the committee, the committee chair and the president decided not to offer the provost position to any of the interviewed candidates and to cancel the search.

Although this process was frustrating for President Glenn, it also was embarrassing for the four interviewed candidates, all of whom were found unacceptable for the position. Other than the president, the provost at Pendel is the most important administrative and academic leader, and President Glenn knows it is critical to fill this position very soon. She is convinced that the open meetings law in her state was a major factor in Pendel's failure to hire an outstanding provost.

Now that President Glenn has cancelled this search for a provost, she has to decide how she will proceed in her determination to attract an outstanding leader to the position. Here are some options the president may consider.

SOME OPTIONS FOR ADDRESSING THIS ISSUE

1. President Glenn strongly resents the application of the open records law to searches for faculty and academic administrators and feels it is an unjustified and unnecessary burden for Pendel University. Moreover, she is not convinced that the public is being well served by the application of this law, as she believes it hinders the university's effort to attract outstanding academic scholars and leaders to the institution. Thus, in this option, President Glenn decides to file a legal challenge to the law, arguing that it should not apply to campus searches for faculty and academic administrators other than the president. She has the support of the alumni association, the faculty senate, her own board of trustees, and some members of the state's legislature for initiating this legal action. While she knows that the previous legal challenge was rejected by the state's supreme court, she feels that decision should only apply to presidential searches, and there is no persuasive justification for including other campus academic positions in it. She publicly announces the filing of the lawsuit and, at the same time, tables the search for a new provost.

President Glenn is not naïve and knows this legal challenge may not have a high probability of success; however, she feels she owes this to her institution, not just for this current search process for the provost, but for all future searches. Moreover, she sincerely believes the "public interest" is not being well served by the application of the open records law to searches other than for the president's position. She expects that the press will editorialize strongly against her action, and she will be publicly accused of a "lack of openness in her administration" and "hiding secrets from the public." But she feels this is the right thing to do, and she has always been a fighter. She doesn't like courts making academic policy and she feels obligated to challenge this.

2. President Glenn wants to hire a provost for Pendel and is determined to get this task accomplished search firm. In the public advertisements for the position, candidates will be advised that an external search firm will be working with Pendel in assisting it in securing outstanding candidates for the position. The search firm staff will work closely with President Glenn and the chair of a campus advisory committee she has appointed. The search firm has informed President Glenn that it has the names of several likely candidates and can ensure the names of these candidates will not be shared with anyone until such time as they agree to become final applicants for the position and are invited to the campus for interviews. In this manner, the search firm may help President Glenn attract better candidates for the position while assuring them confidentiality, at least until such time that the candidates have decided to move forward with their interest. Moreover, such a process, President Glenn argues, is within the spirit of the open records law of her state.

President Glenn does not like to pay the substantial fee to the external search firm, not only because of the current financial problems of the university, but for the precedent it may set for future searches. Moreover, she is privately skeptical that any such firm actually knows more about hiring professional academics than she does! She thinks this option may produce the desired outcome, but personally she is not comfortable with it. In public, she announces this new approach and expresses optimism about the search firm's ability to help identify outstanding candidates for the provost's position. As an experienced administrator, she is not at all surprised when members of the media bitterly criticize her action as "subterfuge . . . a sneaky, back door way to get around a law designed to serve the public interest." She also expects some members of the media to file a legal challenge of her action.

3. President Glenn is facing some tough economic issues at Pendel, and in this option, she feels that after the raucous publicity and failed search, she should settle this issue quickly by taking action on her own. To go through another lengthy search process again would be divisive and costly, and she wants to avoid it. Thus, in this option, President Glenn, after quietly consulting with her own board of trustees, a few faculty, and some of her deans, decides to appoint an interim provost, who is currently the dean of the arts and sciences college at Pendel. This dean is highly respected, and President Glenn knows the dean will do an excellent job as the interim provost. The appointment will be for one calendar year, after which time a new search will be take place for a permanent provost. In her own mind, President Glenn hopes the new interim provost will do such an outstanding job in the position that the interim provost might become appointed to the permanent position.

By taking this action, president Glenn can successfully "defuse" the controversy over the provost search process quickly and move on with important campus issues needing the attention of a new provost. In tapping her most able and respected college dean for the interim position, she is showing everyone that she is in charge and has taken decisive action. She has confidence in this dean for the position, but she knows that some of her critics will be unhappy with her for what they call "backing away" from the issue and for being a "weak administrative leader." But the president feels that there has been far too much energy and attention given to the provost's search, and this option will enable her and the institution to move ahead in a positive manner. Of course, the arts and sciences college dean may think he is not enhancing his professional career by, in effect, taking a position where most people may view him as merely a temporary solution to a problem.

4. President Glenn, in this option, convinces herself that the open records law is a reality in her state and in her university that it is not going to disappear, and she has to learn to cope with it and turn it into an asset not a liability. Thus, she appoints another search committee and admonishes them to go forward with their assignment of attracting excellent candidates to the campus for the provost's position. She also announces publicly that "the open records law in her state is a benefit to the people and to the university, as it encourages and attracts strong candidates—educational leaders who are not afraid of having themselves publicly and rigorously evaluated." She states further that the very nature of the provost's position is open and public, and anyone in such a position is constantly being challenged. She does not want any timid candidates who are unwilling to under-

***go such public scrutiny in order to get the job. She gives the new
search committee 6 months to complete the process.***

President Glenn is being pragmatic with this option. She decides it
is her job as a leader to make things work within the constraints that
she faces. Of course, this new search process may not produce a better set of candidates than the last one did, which could prove embarrassing for her and the university. But with her public statements about
what she expects for the position, she thinks some stronger candidates
may decide to pursue it. If the search is successful, she knows she will
have demonstrated to her colleagues at Pendel, to her own board of
trustees, and to her fellow presidents of the other public universities in
her state that they can, in fact, compete in the open national market
for the best academic talent.

QUESTIONS THAT MAY AID IN THE DISCUSSION
OF THIS CASE STUDY

1. To what extent, if any, should the current dismal economic situation
   at Pendel University drive what President Glenn decides to do?
2. How likely is it that the press' interest in academic searches at
   Pendel will continue? Is it possible that the press will discover that
   their readers do not really care to know about any of these searches
   except one for president?
3. If, in Option 1, Pendel is successful in court and is able to conduct
   its nonpresidential academic searches without regard to the open
   records law, will this result in negative perceptions of the university
   by the public? Is it worth it to risk being accused constantly by the
   press of being secretive?
4. Is an open records law such an actual hindrance to some public universities that some outstanding academic scholars and leaders may
   simply avoid public institutions in favor of private universities?

Suggested Readings Related to This Case

Brodie, Keith H., & Banner, Leslie. (2005). *The Research University Presidency in the Late
Twentieth Century.* Westport, CT: Greenwood Press.
Hochel, Sandra, & Wilson, Charmaine E. (2007). *Hiring Right: Conducting Successful
Searches in Higher Education.* San Francisco: Jossey Bass.

Vick, Julia Miller, & Heiberger, Mary Morris. (2001). *The Academic Job Search Handbook*. Philadelphia: University of Pennsylvania Press.

Vicker, Lauren A., & Royer, Harriette J. (2005). *The Complete Academic Search Manual: A Systematic Approach to Successful and Inclusive Hiring*. Sterling, VA: Stylus Press.

A GRADUATION ISSUE AT
DEJONG UNIVERSITY

SUMMARY OF THE CASE

DeJong University, a prestigious public research university located in the upper Midwest, enrolls almost 35,000 students, of which 22,000 are undergraduates. Competition to gain admission to DeJong is intense, and there are almost eight applicants for each spot in the entering freshman class. A new provost has just been hired at DeJong from another similar institution in the Northeast, and among the several problems she faces is keen frustration among undergraduates (and their parents) about the unavailability of basic classes and, especially, the lack of helpful academic advising. This has resulted in most undergraduates taking almost 5 years to earn their degrees, which is of growing concern to the president, the governing board, and the state legislature.

A DESCRIPTION OF DEJONG UNIVERSITY

DeJong University was founded in 1869 and is one of the most well-known public, land-grant research universities in the nation. It has 11 undergraduate colleges and professional schools of medicine, law, veterinary medicine, and dentistry. It has been a member of the Association of American Universities since the 1950s and prides itself on the ground-breaking research done on its campus for many years, especially in the fields of agriculture, chemical engineering, and molecular biology. The institution is considered a tremendous asset to its state, and the state legislature has been very supportive of its programs.

The president of DeJong is Paul Vandenburg, a distinguished biologist who has been in his position for 8 years. He has been very successful in raising money from private sources and also has been effective in gaining support from the state legislature. He is active in several national educational and governmental activities and is frequently
away from the campus. He is not well known to students and to most
faculty, but he is respected and admired by most of them. The internal administration of DeJong has traditionally been the purview of the
provost, and the various vice presidents of the institution report to the
president through the provost. John Reynolds, who had been the
provost during the past 8 years, recently left to accept the president's
position at another research university, so President Vandenburg was
pleased when he was able to attract Nancy Hunt to DeJong as its new
provost. Her academic discipline is physics, and she had been serving
as dean of arts and sciences at a prestigious Northeastern research university before she was recruited to come to DeJong as its provost.

DeJong University not only has an outstanding academic reputation
and research program, it also has a popular athletic tradition. Its football and men's basketball programs are frequently the subject of
national attention, and the institution has also enjoyed great success in
women's soccer, track and field, and cross country. Much of the social
life of students at DeJong centers around the sports program.

The institution is located in a city of 50,000 residents and enjoys
mostly amicable relations with the municipal leaders. The city is
known as the "university town" in the state, and is dependent on
DeJong for its livelihood. The board of trustees at DeJong consists of
14 citizens appointed by the governor and works hard to support the
institution's continued prestige and academic excellence. Due to the
strong leadership of President Vandenburg, his predecessors, and the
DeJong University Foundation board, the endowment reached almost
$3 billion in 2007. Reflecting the significant downturn in the economy
beginning in 2008, the endowment decreased in value by almost 20
percent by the fall of 2010. But alumni giving continues to be strong,
and President Vandenburg continues to be optimistic about the future
of DeJong University.

THE STUDENTS AND THE FACULTY

DeJong University has kept its enrollment at 35,000 for the last 20 years and has been able to convince the state legislature and its own governing board that remaining at this size will enable the institution to maximize its teaching, research, and service programs. However, there has been considerable pressure on the university to increase the number of undergraduates as the interest in attending DeJong intensifies over the years. Its 22,000 undergraduates come mainly from within the state, although the institution has been able to convince the state legislature to allow it to continue to admit almost 25 percent of its undergraduates from other states and nations. As a result, DeJong has undergraduates from every state and from dozens of foreign countries. As admission has become more and more competitive in the last 20 years, DeJong's entering freshman class is now among the top five public universities in the nation, as measured by SAT scores and class rank. Its graduate students are equally as impressive, and many of the graduate programs at DeJong are among the best in the country.

Over half of the undergraduates at DeJong live in campus residential facilities, and the others live in private apartments close to the campus. Most of the students come from fairly affluent families, and most expect to go on to graduate or professional schools after earning their undergraduate degrees. Minorities comprise almost 25 percent of the student body. With the substantial endowment at DeJong, the institution has been able to maintain attractive financial aid programs for outstanding students who demonstrate need. Student life is active, with almost 600 student organizations. DeJong has a reputation as an institution where there is too much alcohol abuse, and, despite efforts to change this in recent years, not much success has been achieved. Students attend sports events eagerly, and much of the social life at DeJong centers around big football weekends and home basketball games. Undergraduate students at the institution are granted a great deal of independence in selecting their course work, and campus-wide general education requirements have largely been discarded and now are under the purview of each of the colleges. Students, upon admission, are required to select an academic major, which assigns them to one of the colleges. However, it is reasonably easy for undergraduates to change their academic majors, and by the middle of their second year at DeJong, almost half of them have done so.

The faculty at DeJong can be described as highly competent, specialized, and international. They have been recruited from top graduate schools and other prestigious universities and receive good support at DeJong for their research interests. Teaching loads are modest, usually a maximum of two courses per semester or three courses per academic year to increase opportunities to do their research. Faculty are expected to collaborate with their colleagues, especially in the fierce national competition for research grants. DeJong's faculty have been highly successful in attracting external funds to support research programs, especially in medicine, engineering, and biology, and in 2009, the faculty was responsible for obtaining more than $500 million in research funds.

With more than one-third of the students at DeJong being in graduate and professional programs, the faculty are mainly oriented to students studying for these degrees. Most of the faculty also teach undergraduates, although many of them view this as an unattractive distraction from their main academic and research work. Almost 60 percent of the classes that first-year undergraduates take at DeJong are taught by graduate teaching and research assistants and by adjunct faculty. For example, almost all of the sections of the basic calculus course for first-year students are taught by graduate assistants.

The faculty at DeJong are primarily focused on their own academic departments and colleges, and they pay little attention to campus-wide governance issues unless they feel they are being directly affected. Each of the colleges, and especially the advanced graduate programs, are largely independent and handle their own issues. Competition at DeJong for earning tenure and promotion is intense, and faculty know their research and teaching will be closely scrutinized and evaluated based on national standards in their fields. The "up or out" policy in 7 to 8 years is well known among new faculty at DeJong, and this places a great deal of pressure on them.

THE ISSUE FOR THIS CASE STUDY

When Provost Hunt came to DeJong, she knew she would be facing some difficult challenges. Although the university enjoys an outstanding academic reputation and is internationally known for its successful research programs, the institution is facing some serious financial issues due to the continuing economic recession. Support from the legislature is down, and the value of the endowment has also decreased. Students' families have experienced job losses, and this has resulted in demands for more financial support from DeJong. Faculty have not received a salary increase for the past 2 years, and Provost Hunt is fully aware that even in the current academic market, the best of her faculty are likely to receive more attractive offers from competitive institutions eager to bolster their prestige and research capability.

Provost Hunt, considered an expert on academic organization, previously served as dean of arts and sciences at another large research university in the Northeast before coming to DeJong. In her previous role, she was able to reduce the number of academic departments in arts and sciences from 26 to 17 by combining some overly specialized academic programs with others and by discontinuing three departments that had not been attracting many students for several years. Indeed, it was this reorganizational accomplishment on Dr. Hunt's part that was among the talents that made her attractive to President Vandenburg at DeJong. Although he is not involved in the day-to-day internal affairs at DeJong, he is an experienced and insightful academic leader, and he is aware of most of the difficult issues that Provost Hunt will face in her role as the new provost.

The new provost immediately drew some attention when she came to DeJong, as she announced that she was open to new ideas and intended to be a good listener to those on and off campus about campus academic issues. She quickly became aware that the governing board and the state legislature were irritated that DeJong undergraduates take an average of almost 5 years to earn their degrees, and Provost Hunt expressed embarrassment about this fact given the high academic quality of the students. As she looked into this issue more closely, she also became aware that parents of students had been complaining to the institution for several years about the unavailability of some undergraduate classes, and especially the lack of academic advising from faculty for their sons and daughters. This matter was strongly confirmed when Provost Hunt met with student affairs staff, with leaders of the DeJong student government association, and with members of the institution's parents council, an advisory group.

Provost Hunt, who is good at examining problems in universities, decides to look more closely at the problem of why students are taking more than 4 years to graduate. She knows this is unjustifiable to the governing board and the legislature and does not serve the academic or financial interests of either the students or the institution well. She finds that no one is paying much attention to the problem, the 11 colleges are acting independently, people in the central academic administration were aware of the problem for years, but chose to ignore it, students received little attention from faculty regarding their course selection, most faculty do not want to serve as academic advisers to freshmen and sophomores and are ill equipped to do so, and no one is monitoring the number of courses for which undergraduate students are registering. She is convinced that this is a serious problem that must be addressed, and that it is her responsibility to fix it. If she ignores it, she knows that the academic reputation of the institution will be damaged eventually and the students will not be well served. She also knows there are many obstacles in her way.

SOME OPTIONS FOR ADDRESSING THIS ISSUE

1. Provost Hunt should announce a new academic policy for all of the 11 colleges at DeJong University, requiring all undergraduates to register for at least 16 academic credits per semester and for the college deans to monitor the academic progress of students to ensure that they are on track to graduate in 4 years. She intends to set a clear expectation for students and faculty that all students are expected to graduate within 4 years. She will require the colleges at DeJong to make sufficient numbers of basic classes available to undergraduates so they can get the courses they need. She will require the various college deans to provide whatever advising services are needed within their current financial resources.

This option for Provost Hunt sends a strong message that there is a new leader on campus! In selecting this option, the provost is purposely avoiding long discussion and debate with the faculty, deans, and various campus committees. She knows from previous experience that asking these groups for advice will likely take months, or even years, and may not end up solving the problem. She would rather put up with the criticism she knows she will receive from her deans and the faculty than have them get bogged down in an endless debate on this matter. She knows what the problem is and how to solve it, and she knows her president expects her to get this fixed. She also would greatly prefer to spend her time as provost on improving the academic and research programs at the institution. She considers this essentially as an irritating mechanical, administrative issue, one that can and should be quickly solved. But she is also aware that the college deans and the faculty will object to her "unilateral"action, that the deans will complain about lack of resources to carry out her wishes, and that undergraduate students may object to what they consider too heavy an academic course schedule.

2. Provost Hunt is new to DeJong and knows that she will need the support of her college deans and the faculty to accomplish her goals of advancing the academic and research programs at the university. Although she is confident that she knows what needs to be done to solve this issue, she does not want to antagonize her colleagues on the campus or earn a reputation as a provost who is autocratic and not sensitive to the traditions of collegiate governance at DeJong. Thus, this option has Provost Hunt coming to the faculty senate (which includes the deans of the 11 colleges) and announcing that she has become aware of this serious problem that demands the attention of the deans, faculty, student affairs, and student leaders. She announces further the appointment of a special task force whose role it will be to recommend ways that DeJong University can graduate students within 4 years while making needed courses readily available and making good academic advising a reality. She also announces the members of the task force and indicates that it has 6 months to study the problem and make its recommendations to her.

By taking this option, Provost Hunt wants to send a message that this is a serious issue and she has confidence that inviting input from the campus community will not only provide positive results but will confirm her as a new academic leader committed to a genuinely collegiate form of decision making. She is not naïve about the fact that appointing such a task force has some risks, among them that she may receive recommendations that require financial resources that are not available, and even anger from the colleges that their academic auton-omy is being violated. She also knows that such a task force may become a well-publicized forum for all sorts of complaints from facul-ty and students and may become incapable of reaching any meaning-ful recommendations that apply equally and equitably to all 11 of the colleges.

3. Provost Hunt has extensive experience at large, prestigious research universities, is not naïve about the priorities of faculty at such institu-tions, and knows it will be extremely difficult to divert their attention and time from their research activities and their graduate students. Moreover, she knows faculty are quite cynical in their own knowledge that they are only rewarded professionally for their research accom-plishments, not their advising work with undergraduate students. She also knows that academic advising simply is not being done and that first- and second-year students are essentially on their own in the selection of their classes. From her previous experience, she is aware that many other prestigious research universities have established cen-tralized academic advising centers on their campuses, staffed with professionals committed to this activity. Thus, in this option, Provost Hunt decides to meet with her 11 college deans, describing the prob-lem that they already know but have chosen to ignore, and announces to them that she will establish a centralized academic advising center for freshmen and sophomores, and that it will be financed by an assessment from each of their budgets. In collaboration with the vice president for student affairs, each of the eight departments in that division will also be taxed to support the new center, which will then jointly report to the provost and vice president for student affairs. The academic advising center will be responsible for helping all first- and second-year students at DeJong select their courses, advise them about their majors, and monitor their course work and their progress to graduation in the expected 4 years.

By taking this option, Provost Hunt indicates clearly to the deans what it is she intends to do and requires them to help solve the prob-lem, primarily by taxing each of their budgets. She is also openly admitting that academic advising is not taking place, that first- and sec-ond-year students are being shortchanged, and that academic advising for these students is no longer a primary responsibility of the faculty. She will surely receive objections from her deans about their budgets, especially for a program they feel will divert needed funds away from more important priorities, such as faculty salaries and research programs. The faculty reaction to being "relieved" of the academic advising responsibility for first- and second-year students most likely will be muted; they knew they were not doing it anyway and were not committed to it, but they also may feel that a new group of academic advisers, whatever their training may be, cannot possibly offer the same professional advice that "real" faculty can. Moreover, the faculty may view an academic advising center as an unnecessary and expensive addition to an already overly bureaucratic institution. Finally, the provost, by making the new academic advising center jointly responsible to her and to the vice president for student affairs, may find objection from the college deans that they are being required to fund a student service program that should be supported only by the student affairs division.

4. Provost Hunt, although an experienced and knowledgeable academic leader, is keenly aware of the serious problems the institution is facing during this difficult economic recession. She knows her highest priority as provost at DeJong University is to enhance the quality of the academic and research programs. While she is concerned and embarrassed about the extra time that DeJong students take to earn their undergraduate degrees, in this option, she does not want to focus her first major action as provost on an issue the faculty and academic deans do not consider important, at least in comparison with other issues they are facing. So, Provost Hunt decides to take her time with this issue, and after some quiet discussions with her deans and key faculty, she will invite a team of three outside consultants to the campus next summer to evaluate the problem and make recommendations to her. These consultants would consist of an academic dean, a provost, and a retired president, all from similar research institutions.

In taking this option, Provost Hunt is essentially setting aside this issue for a year, giving herself more time and also making sure that she focuses her attention on academic, research, and financial issues of the greatest importance to the institution. She does not want the faculty or the academic deans to get the impression that her highest priority at DeJong will be first- and second-year undergraduate students and their choice of their majors! Such concerns are viewed by most faculty at DeJong as secondary, or ones that less prestigious institutions should deal with. However, she knows this problem will not go away, and it is likely that student complaints and parent frustration will increase until something is done. Finally, she knows first- and second-year students will continue to get poor or no advising concerning their academic programs and that they will take 5 years to graduate.

QUESTIONS THAT MAY AID IN THE DISCUSSION OF THIS CASE STUDY

1. Where is President Vandenburg on this issue? Even though he has essentially turned over the internal administration of academic and research programs at DeJong to Provost Hunt, to what extent should she seek advice and direction from him? If she does seek such direction from the president, is she revealing herself as a meek or an indecisive leader? How confident can she be in her first year to handle this matter on her own?

2 How extensive a role should the 11 deans of the colleges have on this matter? Should Provost Hunt simply expect their support and proceed as she sees fit, or should she be more cautious, consulting them over time, and trying to build a sense of shared responsibility and community among the deans? Over the past many years, the deans have been competitive with one another for resources and value their own independence. They are cordial with each other in public, but they vigorously protect their own academic priorities. Previous provosts at DeJong have not been willing to take strong action in opposition to the college deans; provost Hunt is aware of this and senses that the college deans would like to test their new provost.

3. What should the role of the faculty at DeJong be on this issue? In effect, they feel they are being unfairly blamed for the shortcomings of academic student advising and for the embarrassing length of time it takes undergraduates to earn their degrees. Provost Hunt does not want to alienate herself from the faculty, especially during

her first few months at the institution, but she also knows the faculty considers the advising of first- and second-year students something beneath their academic dignity. She also knows they will react with shock and anger if Provost Hunt makes a decision on this issue without carefully consulting them.

4. How confident can Provost Hunt be in what might eventually emerge from a task force or a consultant's report on this issue? By exercising either of these options, is she taking an unwise risk of exposing this embarrassing problem to the public? It is quite possible that negative publicity might come from the public discussion that will take place, and this might result in demands for staff, services, and support that the institution cannot afford at this time.

Suggested Readings Related to This Case

Bok, Derek. (2003). *Our Underachieving Colleges.* Princeton, NJ: Princeton University Press.

Bright, David, & Richards, Mary. (2001). *The Academic Deanship: Individual Careers and Institutional Goals.* San Francisco: Jossey-Bass.

Cohen, Arthur. (1998). *The Shaping of American Higher Education: Emergence and Growth of the Contemporary System.* San Francisco: Jossey Bass.

Martin, James, & Samuels, James. (2000). *First Among Equals: The Role of the Chief Academic Officer.* Baltimore: Johns Hopkins University Press.

Tucker, Allan, & Bryan, Robert. (1991). *The Academic Dean: Dove, Dragon, or Diplomat?* (2nd Ed.). Washington, DC: American Council on Education.

A PROPOSED NEW HONORS PROGRAM AT WERNER STATE UNIVERSITY

SUMMARY OF THE CASE

Werner State University is a large, public university located in the Midwest. It was founded in 1955 and enrolls 14,000 students. Located in a large city, it mainly serves students from within the city and state. Werner offers some graduate degrees, but more than 90 percent of its students are undergraduates, about half of whom are enrolled on a part-time basis. A faculty committee appointed by the provost was asked to review the undergraduate curricula at Werner State, mainly to address two major problems: declining applications and increasing numbers of students transferring to other institutions before completing their degrees at Werner State. After almost 6 months of study, the committee submitted its report to the provost, and its most prominent recommendation was to create a new honors program at the university. Shortly after receiving the report, a vigorous debate ensued on the campus regarding the proposed honors program. The provost is listening and must decide how she will respond to this recommendation.

A DESCRIPTION OF WERNER STATE UNIVERSITY

Werner State University was established by the state legislature in 1955, when college enrollments were expanding rapidly and a demand for an urban-based public institution in this large city was made by city leaders. There are five older public universities in the state, all located in much smaller cities. When legislative support was secured for the new institution in 1955, it marked a positive step forward in the state's effort to extend educational opportunities to more

120

young people. For many years, residents of the state's largest city had complained that public higher education was not easily accessible or affordable to them, as students had to leave home to attend a public college.

By almost any measure, Werner State has succeeded in its goal of making higher education more accessible to students in its city and area. Its growth has made it the fourth largest public university in its state. The university now offers extensive undergraduate degrees in its five colleges. The deans of the five colleges all report to the provost. The most popular academic majors for undergraduates in 2010 are psychology, business administration, nursing, biology, and education.

Werner State University is governed by its own board of trustees, appointed by the governor of the state. The members are mostly business and professional leaders from the city and are dedicated to the institution.

Werner State prides itself on being an institution that serves a diverse population and on being a welcoming university, especially for first-generation students and minorities. Most students who apply for admission are accepted, and there are extensive academic support programs for underprepared students.

Thomas Armstrong has been the president of Werner State for the past 5 years. He grew up in the city, graduated from Werner State, and, after serving in a number of faculty and academic leadership positions at similar public urban universities, was hired in 2005 to lead the institution. He is highly regarded by students and faculty and is among the most visible public figures in the city. He is a champion for educational opportunity and is an outspoken advocate for Werner State University in the state legislature.

Werner State, established as an urban, commuter-based institution, has gradually assumed some aspects of more traditional universities in recent years. In response mainly to student requests, there are now six residence halls on campus, housing almost 1,800 students, and there are extensive on-campus student support services as well. A campus-wide recreation center was added in 1990 after a campus student union was built in 1983. There is also an intercollegiate athletic program, and football was added in 1975. The university competes in division III sports and does not award athletic scholarships. President Armstrong is an enthusiastic supporter of the athletic program, being convinced that it provides more visibility for the institution among the public and also helps rally the students around their university.

Werner State University is the youngest of the public institutions in its state and has had to struggle since it was founded to secure equitable funding with the more established state universities. It does not yet have the traditions, numbers of prominent alumni, and academic prestige that some of the other public universities in its state have enjoyed for years. But due to its location in the biggest population center of the state, it has the largest legislative delegation, and President Armstrong is confident that his institution will receive better financial support in the future.

THE STUDENTS AND THE FACULTY

The undergraduate students at Werner State are diverse. Most of them are either from the city or from suburbs and locations closeby. The great majority are first-generation students, and most are recipients of state and federal financial aid programs. They view Werner State as their best and most affordable chance to earn a higher education degree and to obtain a job in their field of interest. Most of them continue to live at home while they attend Werner State, and many of them are employed part time in the city at the same time.

While Werner State is officially an open admissions institution, most of the entering freshmen were in the top half of their high school graduating classes. The graduation rate is predictably low–less than 40 percent over a 6-year period–but with improved student counseling and support services in the past several years, the rate has been increasing.

Almost 2,000 Werner State students choose to live on campus in six residence halls built in the early 1990s. This on-campus student population has encouraged a more active student life at Werner State, as has the addition of a recreation center and a student union. As a result, there are more than 150 student organizations, and each year the campus student life appears to be more like traditional universities.

Because so many students work while they are enrolled at Werner State, many of them are enrolled on a part-time basis and, obviously, take longer to graduate. The student affairs offices on campus have made special facilities available for commuter and part-time students, have extended office hours until night, and have encouraged these students to get more involved in campus life.

There is a student government organization at Werner State, and it has struggled to involve the many part-time students while trying to be responsive to their needs. The student government association has mainly focused on increased social activities on the campus and also has sponsored a lively and popular speaker's program. On occasion, it also has become involved in social and political issues in the city.

The financial aid office may be the busiest and most important service office on the campus for Werner State students. Through extensive grant, work-study, and loan programs, most student are recipients of student aid and would not be able to attend the university without it. The university has not been active in fundraising and has a small endowment. President Armstrong is concerned about this and knows privately raised funds must be used to augment state and federal financial aid to students. He is concerned about the growing dependence of students on loans to complete their education.

In the 55 years since its founding, Werner State graduates have mainly accepted jobs in the large city where the institution is located, but more and more of them are moving to other states in 2010, especially those earning degrees in business administration. Werner State graduates have become successful leaders in the city, and the institution prides itself on the number of its graduates who enter teaching and social service fields.

Because the large city in which the university is located offers so much to do, it is both an attraction and a distraction for students. It is an easy bus ride to cultural, athletic, entertainment, and social activities in the city. All of these opportunities make it more difficult, however, to create a campus student life program, as most students love the city and its various attractions. The recreation center and student union have been welcome additions to Werner State, keeping more of them on campus. The students like their Werner State athletic teams, but attendance at the various events is low, although the addition of a men's ice hockey team a few years ago has become quite popular.

There are about 1,500 graduate students at Werner State, and these students come from a variety of institutions. The university currently only offers doctorates in education, psychology, and history, but it hopes to expand its advanced graduate programs to other areas, anticipating more favorable economic conditions in the state and nation in the future.

The graduate students include almost 300 international students, mostly from Asia and Africa, and their presence has enhanced the culture of the campus. The most popular graduate programs are those granting master's degrees in education, business administration, and social work.

Many graduate students work full time while completing their degrees, and many of them attend their classes at night and on weekends, as Werner State has found this is the most effective way to accommodate graduate students. The graduate students have not formed their own governing association but have supported the student government organization when they want to have their voices heard on any issue or problem.

The faculty at Werner State University are attracted to the institution for its commitment to teaching and for its focus on first-generation students. Faculty teach fairly heavy loads each semester and also spend extensive time as academic advisers and mentors to undergraduates. Increasing numbers of faculty are engaged in research and are encouraged to submit grants to support their research efforts. Many of the original faculty at Werner State are now retired, and some of them are concerned that the newer faculty are not as dedicated to helping first-generation undergraduates as they were. The faculty hired in the past 15 years are more research oriented than their predecessors but are not as diverse as a group. Many of the early faculty at Werner State were natives of the city and were not actively involved in their national professional and academic disciplines. The current faculty have come to Werner State from other states and nations and are quite engaged in their profession. However, almost all of them accepted their faculty positions at Werner State because they are committed to teaching undergraduates, especially such a diverse group of first-generation students in an urban setting.

The faculty senate at Werner State has been quite active over the years and has assumed an important role in the decision-making processes of the institution. President Robinson, in particular, consults with them on a regular basis and actively participates in their discussions. Most of their concerns over the past several years have focused on the need for more academic support services for students, more teaching assistantships for graduate students, and the need for more aggressive recruiting of students. Since the recession of 2008, the faculty senate has shifted its attention to faculty salaries, potential reductions in academic programs, and declining student applications.

THE ISSUE TO BE ADDRESSED IN THIS CASE STUDY

Werner State's provost, Dorothy Tubbs, was hired by President Robinson in 2007. She is a chemist and had been the dean of arts and sciences at another large urban institution located on the West Coast. She is highly regarded by faculty and the deans of the five colleges at Werner State for being a forward-thinking and decisive academic leader.

When Provost Tubbs began her duties at Werner State, she was immediately concerned with two difficult problems: declining applications for the freshman class and increasing numbers of students leaving Werner State before they finished their degrees. She suspected that the economic crisis in the country was mainly responsible for these problems. Before taking any specific actions, she felt she needed to examine these issues in more depth.

She worked with faculty colleagues, deans, and student affairs staff at Werner State and set up a series of informal discussions with students, alumni, high school counselors, and admissions staff. What she learned convinced her that more than just the poor economy was contributing to Werner State's problems. The messages were clear: The institution is perceived as an unexciting place to attend, it has little academic rigor, and an undergraduate degree from Werner State is not perceived by students as valuable as one from other institutions. Because these messages were consistently stated by the various groups in the planned discussions, Provost Tubbs took them seriously. She knew these characterizations did not apply to all students, but even if they were accurate for some, she knew some action was needed.

She also became aware that some of the passion felt by the original faculty on the campus for Werner State's dedication to first-generation students had faded. Although she is favorably impressed with the faculty, she knows that some of them are increasingly impatient with teaching students who come to Werner State in need of special academic support. Moreover, the deans of the five colleges at the university are concerned that they may have to eliminate some of their academic programs due to anticipated cutbacks in funding from the state legislature. She has had to put a freeze on new faculty hiring for the past 18 months, and she worries that the budgetary situation at Werner State will get worse in the next 2 years.

In response to these serious concerns, and with the approval of President Robinson, Provost Tubbs appointed a special faculty committee to study and review the undergraduate programs at Werner State, with a particular focus on the declining applications and increasing numbers of students leaving the institution before they graduate. The committee included faculty from each of the colleges, as well as representatives from the alumni, the admissions office, and student affairs. Provost Tubbs worked closely with the faculty senate in selecting the committee members.

The committee worked hard to address the issues it was asked to review. But their major recommendation was not anticipated by Provost Tubbs or the academic deans and the president: The committee suggested that Werner State should create an honors program for undergraduates. The committee argued that an honors program would attract better students, increase the applicant pool, and upgrade Werner State's academic reputation. This, in turn, would make it more likely that current students at the institution would elect to stay until graduation instead of transferring to another college or university. Finally, the committee suggested that an honors program would not require any new funds but could be established by using current faculty, who would design a special curriculum and upgrade the content of designated courses. The committee acknowledged in its report to the provost that this was a rather unusual recommendation but emphasized that it felt Werner State needed to do something quite dramatic to change its image with prospective and current students.

The provost has received the report and has shared it with President Robinson, the college deans, and the other vice presidents at Werner State. The recommendation for a new honors program has caused considerable discussion and debate at the institution. Provost Tubbs, after publicly thanking the committee for their work, knows she has to respond to their recommendation. The following are some options she may consider.

SOME OPTIONS FOR ADDRESSING THIS ISSUE

1. Work to make the proposed honors program a reality to enhance the attractiveness of Werner State University.

Provost Tubbs, initially surprised and skeptical about the committee's recommendation for a new honors program, decides to listen more carefully to the idea and expands the discussion to include the faculty senate, the college deans, and, of course, the president. Werner State is facing a budget crisis, but it is also experiencing a drop in applications and too many students who are leaving the institution. Thus, the provost feels that a proposal for an honors program may revitalize the undergraduate offerings at Werner State and could encourage students from stronger academic backgrounds to apply. She also thinks that such a visible commitment to an honors program might elevate the university's public image and encourage already enrolled students to remain at the institution until they complete their studies. The committee's proposal reflects careful work on their part and includes specific models for various curricula that might become part of an honors program. It also suggests a way that such a program could be offered only 1 year from now and argues that it will not require any additional faculty or funding. Provost Tubbs, as a former dean herself, is not naïve about the potential conflicts an honors program might create among the colleges and is also worried about the idea of academic elitism conflicting with the objectives of Werner State's commitment to first-generation students. But after a thorough discussion with President Robinson, she decides that it is worth pursuing the honors program idea, at least on a pilot basis. She is willing to take this risk because she has been convinced that Werner State is in trouble, and the institution needs to take some unusual actions to revitalize itself.

The provost is likely to encounter considerable resistance from the college deans in this plan for an honors program, as they will be concerned about who will be in charge of it, how faculty will be assigned to it, how teaching loads will be affected, and where it will be housed. She will inform them that their budgets will not be reduced, and that only faculty interested in teaching honors courses will be included. She is confident that faculty in many academic disciplines will be interested in doing this, and because of the small number of students likely to be part of the program in its first year, she thinks she can make this work. She has an associate provost in her office who will assume responsibility for the honors program who is already working with the admissions office to announce it. This associate provost is working closely with a special faculty committee representative of the colleges to identify specific courses students will be able to select as members of the honors program. Plans are to attract 150 freshmen students to the program in the first year, and it is hoped that the publicity for the program might attract some potential donors interested in supporting it with scholarship dollars. Finally, the provost knows that President Robinson's support for this pilot honors program is critical and that he will certainly have to defend this unusual action to the board of trustees. She is prepared to assist him in this regard!

2. Convert an existing residence hall as the "Werner State Honors Hall" and establish this hall as the home for an honors program.

In her conversations with various administrators, faculty, and students about the committee's recommendation for an honors program, the provost becomes convinced that the most effective way to create a successful program is to give it a visible and prestigious place on the campus. Thus, she worked closely with the student affairs vice president at Werner State, and they decided to convert one of the existing residence halls into the home of the honors college. An office would be placed there, and the current resident adviser apartments would be modified to include space for three faculty masters who would live in the facility for up to a year to serve as mentors and advisers for the students. Students would be recruited not only to the academic honors program at Werner State but also to this specially designated honors hall. The provost and student affairs vice president believe that such a facility would be attractive to new students and that its presence on the campus would contribute positively to campus life. If this plan is successful, the provost anticipates that the 400-student residence hall will be filled with honors students in the next 3 years. There will be some fairly modest costs involved in converting the residence hall to an honors hall, but these will be absorbed by the housing division, which, as an auxiliary, does not receive any state funds. Finally, the provost believes that giving the new honors program this kind of visibility on the campus will send a message to the public and the faculty that this is important to Werner State and that it represents an exciting new academic opportunity for prospective students.

Provost Tubbs, with the encouragement of her student affairs vice presidential colleague, believes that this new honors residence hall will become an incentive to become a part of the honors program. Both plan to give this converted honors hall a prominent place in the campus tours for prospective students and display it on the university's website. They also will ask admissions staff to talk about it with high school counselors and the parents of prospective students. The provost knows that this idea will be new to Werner State, and the notion of a special residence hall for honors students may be viewed as unfair to other students. She has enlisted the support of the student affairs staff to work closely with enrolled Werner State students to help make this honors hall and honors program a success. She believes the current students will be convinced that this change will be exciting and may give more perceived value to their own degrees. Despite the economic problems facing the state and the institution, the provost feels she needs to introduce some fairly dramatic and visible changes at Werner State that will revitalize the academic culture of the institution.

3. Receive the committee report and ask the university's curriculum council to explore the proposal for an honors program in more detail and to make its recommendations via the faculty senate to the provost.

In this option, the provost is quite skeptical about the idea, and especially about its timing, given the economic problems being faced by Werner State. But as provost, she had asked a faculty committee to think seriously about the undergraduate programs at her institution, and specifically about what might be done to attract more applicants and decrease the numbers of students leaving before graduation. She feels it would be inconsiderate and unfair simply to reject the proposal without further study. The university's curriculum council is perhaps the most influential standing committee of the faculty senate, and she believes the honors program proposal needs to be carefully scrutinized by it. The council includes faculty from each of the colleges, and over a period of the next 6 months, the provost believes the council will give the proposal a fair hearing. If the council should decide to endorse the idea and recommend implementing the honors program, the provost knows she will have a much stronger basis for giving it her support. The curriculum council also includes two student representatives, and their participation in the discussion during the academic year might prove helpful in considering the feasibility of the proposal. In selecting this option, the provost might be accused of trying to avoid making a decision on the honors program proposal and "burying" it in the academic bureaucracy of the institution. Although the provost is impatient and feels a strong need to take some actions that will effectively address the serious problems her university is facing, she thinks engaging the institution in this issue for the next 6 months is necessary before she should take any action.

Members of the original committee worked hard on their proposal, and some of them may feel that any further study of the honors program idea is an unnecessary duplication of their efforts. Thus, the provost will benefit from meeting with the original committee, hearing their concerns, and thanking them for their efforts before she proceeds with this third option. She thinks any publicity about the proposed honors college during the 6 months that the curriculum council discusses it may prove beneficial to the university, which has been too often characterized by the press as "not particularly committed to academic excellence." She meets with the curriculum council and asks the group to consider ways of recruiting and retaining students via the proposed honors program, as she knows that merely announcing that Werner State now has such an opportunity will not be enough to make it a success. She is reasonably confident that the curriculum council will do a good job of evaluating this proposal and that they will present her with a thoughtful recommendation regarding it. Finally, she knows if the council vacillates and gives her a lackluster report, she will have to decide on her own what direction to take.

4. Thank the committee for its work, but reject its recommendation for the proposed honors program.

The provost is responsible for the academic program at Werner State and is facing a daunting set of difficult problems, mostly related to the severe economic situation. Although she is intrigued by the idea of an honors program at Werner State, and even thinks it could possibly revitalize some undergraduate academic curricula, she views it as little more than a luxury to dream about now and something that would not effectively address the problems of declining applications and increasing numbers of students transferring out of Werner State. Thus, she meets with the committee and thanks them for their work but rejects the proposal for the honors program, while leaving the idea open for discussion in future years at the institution. She believes it could operate at cross-purposes with the traditional commitment of Werner State to nonaffluent, first-generation students by introducing an elitist sounding program within the institution. She also knows from her previous experience as an academic leader that honors programs at times only can succeed if they have the support and cooperation of the faculty from all academic disciplines, and that they can become little more than recruiting devices for institutions. If she were to pursue the cre-

ation of an honors program in better economic times, she would insist that it had real academic substance and that it did not enjoy such special academic privileges on the campus that it caused dissention among the faculty. Finally, in rejecting the committee's recommendation for an honors program, the provost should be ready to suggest and implement some new actions that will directly address the institution's problems.

It is not easy for a provost to reject a thoughtful recommendation presented to her by a faculty committee she has appointed, especially if the committee has done its job in a diligent manner. But in this option, the provost feels she cannot accept the idea of the honors program at this time and must share her views candidly with the committee. Of course, she will need to have some other actions she will implement, and hopefully these may be ones the committee, faculty senate, and president can support. The courage she exhibits by rejecting the committee's recommendation will have to be augmented by realistic, results-oriented actions on her part. She may face some embarrassment in receiving the honors program proposal, as some campus critics might feel she should not have been surprised by it and should have made her views known to the committee before they formally submitted it to her. But she feels that if she appoints a high-level faculty committee to consider such a difficult set of issues, they should be free to make whatever recommendations to her they think are appropriate. Because she has now decided not to accept the committee's proposal, she must develop another plan to address the problems at Werner State!

QUESTIONS THAT MAY AID IN THE DISCUSSION OF THIS CASE STUDY

1. If Provost Tubbs decides to implement the honors program at Werner State, how can she persuade her colleagues that it will be compatible with the university's mission of primarily serving first-generation students?

2. To what extent, if any, should the provost involve her president in this matter? She is confident that she has his support, but what should his role be in this proposal for an honors program?

3. If the honors program is implemented and attracts sufficient numbers of students in the next 3 years, will its success result in other undergraduate programs at Werner State to be considered second class?

4. Assume that the provost is actually furious with the committee for presenting her with a recommendation she feels is ill timed and unlikely to solve the problems of declining enrollment and increasing transfers to other institutions. Should she have intervened in this process earlier and prevented the committee from making such a proposal?

Suggested Readings Related to This Case

Ferren, Ann S. (2004). *Leadership Through Collaboration: The Role of the Chief Academic Officer.* Washington, DC: American Council on Education Oryx Press Series on Higher Education.

Friedman, Paul G. & Jenkins-Friedman, Rena C. (1986). Fostering Academic Excellence Through Honors Programs. San Francisco: Jossey Bass.

Martin, James, & Samels, James E. (1997). *First Among Equals: The Role of the Chief Academic Officer.* Baltimore: Johns Hopkins University Press.

Miller, Michael T. (2003). *Improving Faculty Governance: Cultivating Leadership and Collaboration in Decision Making.* San Francisco: Jossey Bass.

A FREE SPEECH INCIDENT AT JURNIGAN STATE UNIVERSITY

SUMMARY OF THE CASE

Jurnigan State University is located in a large city in the Mid-Atlantic region of the United States and enrolls 31,000 students. It has a diverse student body, which includes 3,400 international students. It has extensive graduate programs and schools of law and medicine. There are two private colleges located in the city as well, and there are four other publicly supported universities in the state. Jurnigan State is the largest and most comprehensive institution in the state. In October 2009, the Hillel Student Association invited an Israeli diplomat to speak on campus and was assisted in the event by the Jurnigan student government, who paid half of the speaker's fee from student activity funds. The speech was scheduled in a 300-seat auditorium in an academic building on campus. When the speaker was introduced, about 20 members of the audience stood and began shouting racial epithets at the speaker, making it impossible for him to be heard. These protesters were all wearing T-shirts with "Palestinian Student Organization" written on them. The student president of Hillel, who had introduced the speaker, asked the protesters to be quiet but was ignored. After a period of almost 20 minutes, the campus police were able to escort the protesters from the building, and the speech was delivered. The campus newspaper covered the event, as did a local television station, and the publicity resulted in an uproar, with student, faculty, and community groups threatening one another and making various demands on the university. The vice president for student affairs is responding to this incident.

A DESCRIPTION OF JURNIGAN STATE UNIVERSITY

Founded in 1920, Jurnigan State was the first publicly supported institution of higher education established in the state. Reflecting the relatively small population of the state at the time, its enrollment never exceeded 8,000 students until after World War II. Then as the state's population grew rapidly, Jurnigan State expanded. By 1970, its enrollment was 22,000, and the institution developed new graduate programs and a medical school. By the year 2000, it had become a large, comprehensive research university with a rich diversity of ethnic minorities and international students and faculty. The large city in which Jurnigan State is located is well known as one of the most culturally diverse in the nation.

Jurnigan State University's academic programs in engineering, business administration, law, and public service have received national acclaim in recent years. Several of its graduates have been prominent elected and professional leaders in the state, including the current governor and one U.S. senator. Ten current members of the state legislature are also Jurnigan State graduates. Many of these leaders are graduates of the Jurnigan State law school.

The university has been successful in the past 20 years in encouraging students to become active in community service programs, and service-learning courses have become quite common in many academic departments. Jurnigan State is known as an urban-based institution whose diverse students and faculty are actively involved in social and political action. The activities of its students are often covered in the press, as one student group or another is doing something viewed as outrageous, obscene, or alarming by various members of the public! The institution is sometimes viewed as a diverse microcosm of the larger world, and for the most part, the legislature and the public have been quite tolerant of all the activity.

Jurnigan State is governed by a board of trustees of 12 citizens appointed by the state governor. The current president of the university, Maria Santoro, is a historian who has been in her position for 5 years. She is highly respected in the state for her commitment to equal educational opportunity and her advocacy for poor and disadvantaged citizens. On the campus itself, she is well liked but is not as well known as some previous presidents of Jurnigan State, as she is frequently out of the city, working with the state legislature and in other locations, raising money for the institution. Because Jurnigan State is in a state not as negatively affected by the economic recession of 2008 as some others, it has not had to make significant financial cuts in its programs and is cautiously optimistic about its budget. Jurnigan State is a well-respected public university, and it has aspirations to become one of the nation's top 30 public research universities by 2025.

THE STUDENTS AND THE FACULTY

The undergraduate students at Jurnigan State University come mainly from within the state, and over half of them come from within the city of 2 million where the institution is located. Because the institution now attracts many more applicants than it did just 20 years ago, it is now quite selective, and most of the students in the entering freshman class were in the top 20 percent of their high school class. They are attracted to Jurnigan State because of its location, relatively low cost, cultural diversity, and academic reputation.

Most of the undergraduate students live in the city, although about 2,000 of them live in campus residence halls. Almost 40 percent of the students are minorities, and international students number 3,400. Student life at Jurnigan State is lively, with more than 450 student organizations, representing almost every imaginable political, social, religious, ethnic, and cultural point of view. Intercollegiate athletics are also popular, and football weekends bring thousands of fans to the campus. Because of the tremendous diversity at the university, students are constantly in touch with others from different cultural, religious, racial, and political backgrounds, and most students revel in this atmosphere. Although the rhetoric among all these diverse groups is sometimes raucous, most students enjoy mingling socially with friends from different backgrounds than their own. This diverse cultural experience is considered the primary asset of Jurnigan State by most of its students, and it is a matter of considerable pride within the university.

Jurnigan State has had a reputation since the 1960s as a place where a good deal of social protest takes place, especially about state and national policies regarding race, affirmative action, international issues, and military action. It is also an institution with a tradition of freedom of expression, with some newspapers referring to the campus as its own "Hyde Park." Although the protests have remained relatively calm for the past few years, there were building takeovers and some violence during the Vietnam period, when several students were arrested and suspended from the university.

Most of the undergraduates are serious about their academic programs, and in just the past 10 years, the graduation rate has increased almost 10 percentage points. Now almost 70 percent graduate within 4 years, and more than half of the others eventually earn their degrees within the next 3 years. Since the 2008 recession, more Jurnigan State graduates are continuing their education in graduate and professional schools, but most seek employment in the state and region immediately after earning their undergraduate degrees.

The graduate students at Jurnigan State are even more diverse than the undergraduates and come from most states in the nation and many foreign countries. Although graduate students are not as engaged in social and political action groups as many undergraduates are, they have formed a graduate student union to represent their interests at the university. This union has focused primarily on such issues as compensation for graduate and research assistantships and on their own health insurance costs.

The faculty at Jurnigan State University have been quite stable for several years, as most of them enjoy working at the university and living in a large city known for its good weather and stimulating cultural life. Most faculty come from outside the state and region, and many, especially in agriculture, economics, and engineering, come from outside the country. Faculty at Jurnigan State enjoy good support for their teaching and research from the university, and competition for tenure is quite strenuous. The faculty in recent years have been quite successful in attracting external funds to support their research, although most of this funding supports work in engineering, medicine, and the physical sciences. Faculty in other areas often feel they are disadvantaged in this competition for research support, and this has led to some dissention between "the scientists and the humanists" at the university.

The faculty, although primarily focused on their academic activities in their own departments, pay close attention to university policies through their participation in the faculty senate. Unlike most other large, public universities, where faculty senates are often not very active, at Jurnigan State, the faculty senate is frequently the locus of lively debate about campus programs and issues. The faculty senate is in regular contact with the administration, mainly with the provost concerning academic issues, but also with the vice president for student affairs, Quentin Holtz, about social action political action issues. Although there are often disagreements between the faculty senate and the administration, most of the discussions have remained cordial.

THE ISSUE TO BE ADDRESSED IN THIS CASE STUDY

The Hillel Student Association at Jurnigan State has a meeting house just off the campus, and its membership lists some 350 students, most of whom are Jewish. The house was built in 1962 by Jurnigan State alumni who wanted to create a place where study and social interaction could occur for Jewish students. Only about half of the Jewish students at Jurnigan State are actually members of the Hillel Student Association. Its off-campus house is mainly a comfortable meeting space and a welcoming facility for Jernigan State alumni when they return to campus for various events. The Hillel Student Association is active in student political life, and in the past 5 years, two of its members have been elected to the position of student body president at Jurnigan State.

The Hillel Student Association is well known on campus for its sponsorship of various lectures and seminars, mainly on religious and political issues concerning the Middle East. Jurnigan State has a required student activity fee, and with this fee the student government association administers a speaker's program that makes funds available for campus student groups to invite prominent speakers to Jurnigan State. In a typical academic year, more than 35 such speakers appear on campus and speak on a great variety of topics. The student government association tries hard to be content neutral in its financial sponsorship of speakers. The speaker program is quite popular and, while sometimes controversial, certainly adds to the cultural and intellectual life of students at Jurnigan State.

In October 2009, the Hillel Student Association invited an Israeli diplomat to Jurnigan State to present a lecture on Middle Eastern peace prospects. Half of the speaker's fee was paid by the student government association, with Hillel paying the other half. Not anticipating a large crowd for this event, the student sponsors reserved a 300-seat auditorium in an academic building on campus. Students usually comprise about half of those who attend such events at Jurnigan State, as faculty and interested residents of the city make up the others. About 200 people were in attendance. The student newspaper sent a reporter, and the sponsors were not surprised when they noticed a television cameraperson from the local station there as well. Nothing seemed unusual in the auditorium as the event was about to begin that night when the president of the Hillel Student Association went to the microphone to introduce the guest speaker.

Within the first minute of the introduction, the student president was interrupted by about 20 young men in the auditorium, who began shouting racial epithets so loudly that he was not able to continue. The protesting young men all were wearing T-shirts, on which were printed "Palestinian Student Organization," and they objected to the presence of the Israeli diplomat on the campus. The protesters were asked several times by the event chairman to desist in their boisterous behavior, but they refused to do so. Those in attendance at the event expressed their anger toward the protesters, as they wanted to listen to the speaker. Finally, a student affairs staff member who was present at the event, after also failing to convince the protesters to be quiet, called the campus police. In 20 minutes, the police peaceably removed the protesters, and placed them under arrest for disrupting a university activity, which was also a violation of the campus student conduct code. The speaker was then introduced with no interruption, and the presentation was made with no further incident.

With such a diverse student body, with 3,400 international students, and with its location in a large and cosmopolitan city, students and student groups at Jurnigan State are frequently engaged in various controversial issues. But everyone on campus knows that the institution's commitment to freedom of expression does not include the right to disrupt an event and that there will be consequences for doing so. In this incident involving the Hillel Student Association and the Palestinian Student Organization, well-established disciplinary procedures were followed after the event, and the arrested students were informed that they would be referred to the student judicial office where their cases would be heard by the Dean of Students.

The Palestinian Student Organization (PSO) is 1 of more than 450 student groups that choose to register with the campus activities office.

It lists a membership of about 40 students, many of whom are international students from Arab countries. There are at least 10 other student organizations at Jurnigan State whose focus is on Middle East policy; the PSO is perhaps the most outspoken of these groups. There are also several student "country groups" (e.g., the Afghani Student Association, the Syrian Student Association) whose activities are mainly social in nature. The PSO has not engaged in disruptive action before at Jurnigan State, but it has been outspoken in its disagreement with U.S. support for Israel and of military actions of Israel it considers inhumane.

The student affairs vice president, Quentin Holtz, is a perceptive and outgoing man who is often in personal touch with many student organizations. He is well known on the campus and is viewed as a fair and caring administrator, committed to Jurnigan State's traditions of freedom of expression and appreciation of diversity. He is an advocate of student freedom and genuinely enjoys the dozens of student groups and the lively debates they have. He and his student affairs staff are very visible on campus and are in attendance at hundreds of student events at Jurnigan State.

As soon as the Hillel-sponsored event was over, Holtz learned about the disruption, arrests, and removal of the protesters from one of his staff members who was there and called him at home that night. Holtz was pleased with how the incident was handled and agreed that the student conduct process would proceed regarding the violation of the student conduct code by the protesters.

Holtz wrote an e-mail message to President Santoro that night, making sure she was informed about this incident, as he expected it to be covered in the late evening television news cast. Any time students or others have to be physically removed from a campus event, it always results in television coverage, Holtz knew.

In the next 48 hours, many people at Jurnigan State were surprised when several student groups marched through the campus, advocating various actions—either against the PSO, Hillel, the campus police, or the university administration. The faculty senate called a special meeting to debate whether the action of the university was appropriate, and, in particular, questions were raised about the appropriateness of using required student activity fees to pay for a "biased" Israeli speaker when no such funds were used for speakers representing other points of view. Several students and a few student groups issued statements that it was their intent to disrupt any future lectures that were "obviously an attempt by the university to support Israel." Others threatened that if any disciplinary hearings were to be held against the PSO "martyrs," it was their plan to disrupt them. Additionally, some international groups in the city were highly critical of the university action, and others were critical of Hillel for sponsoring such a speaker. During the next night, the Hillel house was defaced with four swastikas, and a large sign was attached to the house, saying, "Israel must be eliminated." During this time, television news coverage of the various events was extensive, and many students and faculty appeared in interviews conducted by the station. By the end of the week, this incident had not only consumed the Jurnigan State campus with vicious and highly divisive rhetoric, it had become of interest nationally and was now receiving coverage by the network television stations. Worse yet, on this campus where there had been tolerance, mutual respect, and a long tradition of freedom of expression, there was now a fear of violence due to the passionately felt views of so many individuals and groups.

The student affairs vice president, Quentin Holtz, can scarcely believe the turmoil on the campus he loves. As he faces this situation, the following are some alternatives he may consider.

SOME OPTIONS FOR ADDRESSING THIS ISSUE

1. Vice President Holtz is an experienced administrative leader, and he knows his university well. He has witnessed turmoil and disagreements on his campus before, and he does not want to overreact to this situation. Above all, he does not want to escalate the turmoil by antagonizing any of the warring groups. He is fearful that any incident of violence would make this already tense situation much worse. He has good relationships with student groups, and members of his staff are also well known to student leaders. He has been active in the community for several years and feels comfortable talking with leaders in the cultural, religious, business, and professional organizations in the city. In this option, Holtz decides that the most prudent action is to be patient and let all the noise and commotion diminish, which he thinks will happen in about another month. It is now mid-October, and Holtz feels that by the Thanksgiving holiday break, it may cool down, and then, with the university on vacation for a few days and the end of the semester close by in mid-December, the attention of the Jurnigan State community will move on to other things. In the meantime, however, he and his staff will quietly be talking with various student, faculty, and community groups and with individual leaders in an effort to remove some of the hatred and vitriol and to bring some reason and mutual respect to the conversations.

This option assumes that Vice President Holtz has the confidence of his president at Jurnigan State to resolve this issue without more dramatic action. No president likes the negative publicity that results from such an incident, and the president, like Holtz, is fearful of any violence that might occur. Holtz knows he may expose himself and the institution to severe criticism by what some people may view as a weak, laissez-faire approach to this incident, especially because some members of the press have described it as a "breakdown of civility" at the institution. He also knows that by not taking any obvious and overt public actions, he may further antagonize those who are furious at the university for what they feel is its "bias toward Israel." Finally, in this option, he is depending on his years of trust with students and others as a calm and understanding leader to resolve the situation and to do so in a manner consistent with Jurnigan State's tradition of tolerance, patience, and respect for others.

2. This incident at Jurnigan State has exposed some raw emotions and strongly held beliefs that have been simmering just below the surface for a long time. With so many diverse views on volatile issues and with so many groups openly vying with one another, perhaps it was inevitable that a single incident, however small, would incite this orgy of ugly rhetoric, accusations, and threats. In this option, this is the view held by Vice President Holtz, who probably knows and understands as much about the cultural, ethnic, and political life of his campus as anyone does. He is an educator, and he tries to view most situations as teachable moments! Thus, in the option, Vice President Holtz intends to seize this situation as an opportunity for Jurnigan State to come together and examine, criticize, and renew its basic values of tolerance, respect for differences, and freedom of expression. With the president's support and that of the faculty senate and the student government association, Holtz and a group of his staff, some faculty, students, and community leaders, organize a week- long "Jurnigan State University Convocation on Tolerance and Diversity." On the first day, President Santoro will speak to the university community in the large basketball arena, and then faculty will conduct discussions in their classes on the incident throughout the week. Each day, there will be seminars, panel discussions, public debates, and speeches around the campus, and the university's website will be devoted to descriptions of the various contributions that several student, faculty, and community groups have made to the academic community for many years. At the end of the week, a celebratory convocation will be held for the university community, featuring a presentation by a highly respected international civil rights leader. Finally, the convocation will include cultural presentations, music, and dance from some of the many diverse cultural student groups at the university.

In this option, Vice President Holtz is placing his faith in the academic community at Jurnigan State to heal itself. Moreover, he is affirming that an institution has an obligation to demonstrate that, through education itself, the university can set an example to the larger society about how to address the most volatile social and political issues of the time. By choosing this option, Holtz must be able to convince others, including the president, that this week-long convocation deserves their support and participation. Without it, of course, this approach cannot work. He is relying on his ability to persuade others that this is worth the effort and on his ability to organize such a large campus-wide, week-long series of events very quickly. Holtz knows that some people will only be satisfied with public retribution for some groups and favorable praise for others, and that this option probably will not be received well. He also knows that some groups may be so angry and embittered that they will try to sabotage the planned series of events or may simply refuse to participate in them. Finally, he fears that even this sincere attempt to bring people together for civil conversation may actually make the situation worse, with individuals and groups more interested in shouting and accusing than in listening and understanding.

3. Vice President Holtz was a law professor for several years prior to becoming the student affairs vice president and has had extensive experience as a professional mediator and arbitrator. Indeed, it was his success in these activities that made him attractive to Jurnigan State University when he was hired. He is intrigued by the ways individuals and groups sometimes resolve their differences, but he has also been frustrated when they have been unable to do so. Holtz sees many aspects to this volatile situation at his university, but he thinks it is mainly an understandable disagreement between Jewish and Arab students and faculty and that he should offer an opportunity for representatives of these groups to meet with him in mediation sessions, the purpose of which will be to negotiate a formal set of agreements that will guide their interactions on the campus in the future. He will enlist the assistance of two other trained mediators for this process, which will likely take at least a month. By announcing this action, of course, he will need to secure the willingness of representatives of the two groups to participate in the mediation with good faith. Holtz knows that this will require his best persuasive powers! In taking this action, he is also assuming that others in the Jurnigan State community will accept it as a reasonable alternative to their continued noisy rhetoric and threats. Finally, he is relying on his own ability to help forge some kind of civil and enforceable agreement between the representatives of the two groups that not only respects the rights of each group but also serves as a model that the rest of the university will notice and perhaps emulate.

Vice President Holtz knows that this is a way of responding to this series of ugly incidents that is unusual for the academic community. Faculty, students, and academic administrators have traditionally addressed their differences with one another through debate, discussion, and compromise. By opting for a formal mediation process, however, Holtz believes he is providing a realistic and practical method of actually resolving the issue and within a specific time period. He is offering a unique model for resolving differences that requires honest and frank sharing of views, and one that respects and honors differences without any bias or "taking sides." Successful mediation requires time and hard work, and its success depends on the willingness to participate in good faith and to agree to uphold any eventual agreement.

This process also sends a message to the academic community that this is a special and important problem and that a special way of addressing it is needed. Such a mediation panel would need to be assured that, if it can forge an agreement between the representatives of the two groups, such an agreement would be accepted by the president and the governing board of Jurnigan State.

4. Vice President Holtz, after quiet and thoughtful conversation with the president, provost, student body president, chair of the faculty senate, and selected community leaders, decides in this option that this serious situation is so volatile that it must be "defused" at once. Thus, he asks President Santoro to appoint a special task force on "Civility and Freedom of Expression at Jurnigan State University." This task force of 20 people, chaired by a respected retired president of the university, will include faculty, students, and community leaders, and, to the extent possible, it will be representative of the major points of view held by members of the university community. Its charge will be to discuss, examine, and critique the current cultural and political climate at Jurnigan State, and, in accordance with the university's tradition and strong commitment to civility and freedom of expression, to make recommendations to the president to resolve the current crisis and to suggest ways to build a campus climate where divergent views can be expressed, respect for others can be honored, and genuine friendships can be established.

Vice President Holtz and his colleagues recognize the seriousness and volatility of this situation at Jurnigan State and feel that this option may enable the major issues to be addressed in an appropriate forum and also may enable the groups and individuals who hold such strong and divergent views to meet and begin a useful discussion. The task force meetings surely will be difficult, but at least they will demonstrate to the Jurnigan State community that it intends to meet these issues in a forthright manner, and that it is giving this matter the highest priority it can. Holtz knows that this process will take time, that the rhetoric will often be harsh, and that some individuals and groups will be skeptical of it all. But a continuing and mostly civil discussion of these volatile issues, even if it goes on for some months, is far preferable to doing nothing and allowing the anger on the campus to escalate. Holtz and his colleagues know they will have to be persuasive with some individuals and groups to secure their participation in the work of the task force and, eventually, to earn their support for its recommendations.

QUESTIONS THAT MAY AID IN THE DISCUSSION OF THIS CASE

1. Because this incident involved a student-sponsored lecture, the vice president for student affairs assumed the leadership role for the institution in responding to it. Of course, it escalated into a problem that involved almost everyone in the university and even parts of the city. Should the university president university have assumed a more aggressive and public role in this matter?

2. The deeply felt resentment and anger of these groups toward one another did not originate at Jurnigan State University, of course. They are the result of a long history that long preceded the university. Nevertheless, the institution cannot escape them or pretend they can be ignored in its educational and campus life programs and policies. Are there additional resources that Jurnigan State University could use in addressing this difficult set of issues?

3. Attempting to resolve difficult and volatile situations that stem from deep cultural, religious, and cultural differences, what kinds of knowledge and skill do university leaders need? What should their own backgrounds be?

4. When cultural, religious, and political groups clash, the press coverage often becomes a prominent place for many of the issues to be aired. The institution, of course, cannot control this, but what, if anything, can the university do to minimize its impact?

Suggested Readings Related to This Topic

Cheldelin, Sandra I., & Lucas, Ann F. (2003). *Academic Administrator's Guide to Conflict Resolution.* San Francisco: Jossey Bass.

Moran, Robert T., Harris, Phillip R., & Moran, Sarah V. (2007). *Managing Cultural Differences: Global Leadership Strategies for the 21st Century* (7th ed.). Burlington, MA: Butterworth-Heinemann.

Warters, William C. (2008). *Mediation in the Campus Community: Designing and Managing Effective Programs.* San Francisco: Jossey Bass.

Zdziarski, Eugene L., Dunkel, Norbert W., & Rollo, J. Michael. (2007). *Campus Crisis Management: A Comprehensive Guide to Planning, Prevention, Response, and Recovery.* San Francisco: Jossey Bass.

A PROPOSED BACHELOR'S DEGREE AT DAKER COMMUNITY COLLEGE

SUMMARY OF THE CASE

Daker Community College is a publicly supported 2-year institution located in the Midwest. It enrolls 14,000 students in its various pre-transfer, career preparation, and workforce support programs. It was founded in 1962 and is located in a city of 70,000 residents. The state legislature is concerned about the increasing costs of attending the five state universities in the state and is facing questions from voters about why it is so much more expensive to attend a state university than it is to attend a community college. When the economic recession of 2008 occurred, many parents of prospective college students lost their jobs and were worried that they might not be able to send their children to college. The state is facing a shortage of public school teachers, nurses, and other health care professionals. In view of these problems, the higher education committee of the state legislature has drafted a bill that would enable the seven state-supported community colleges to begin offering bachelor's degrees in the fall of 2011. The drafting of this bill immediately resulted in vigorous debate among the presidents of the five state universities, the nine private colleges, and the seven public community colleges in the state. The state-wide coordinating board for higher education and the boards of trustees for the various colleges joined the debate, and questions were raised by the regional accreditation association as well. After additional debate, the bill was forwarded to the full legislature and was passed and signed by the governor. Daker Community College is located in a city that also includes one of the state universities, and their relationship has been close and cooperative for many years. The president of Daker Community College finds herself in the middle of this complicated situation and must decide how her institution should respond to it.

147

A DESCRIPTION OF DAKER COMMUNITY COLLEGE

Daker Community College was established in 1962 in response to proposals made by business, educational, and civic leaders of its region and was granted a charter by the state legislature. It was the second of the public community colleges in the state, with the remaining ones being established in the next 6 years. While the original emphasis in the state's community colleges was on pre-transfer programs, it soon became clear that half their enrollment would consist of students interested in terminal, career preparation programs lasting from 6 weeks to 2 years. Almost by any measure, Daker Community College has been successful. By 1975, its enrollment tripled from its 1965 level, and it continued to grow steadily after that time. Now, in 2010, the enrollment in its various programs totals 14,000. As the population of this region of the state continues to grow, Daker's enrollment is expected to reach 20,000 students by 2020.

Students have been attracted to Daker from the region primarily because of its convenience, low tuition, open access, and broad array of academic and career-oriented programs. After some politically oriented disputes in the 1960s and early 1970s, when community college graduates were not readily welcomed by the state universities as transfers, the state legislature passed an articulation agreement, which greatly eased the ability of students to transfer. It also resulted in better articulation between the community colleges and the several independent 4-year colleges in the state.

Daker is located in a city where one of the state universities has been for 125 years. When the proposal to establish Daker was being discussed back in 1961, leaders of the established state university were not supportive of the idea, because they were concerned that there was not enough money in the state to fund another college, especially given their view that the state universities were not funded adequately. Privately, some of them also felt that the community colleges would dilute the quality of higher education in the state and take some of their students away especially because tuition at the community colleges would be lower than what students have to pay at the state universities.

Daker is truly a community-based college, involving members of its city and surrounding towns in a great variety of academic, professional development, recreational, and cultural programs. In 2010, it teaches classes during the day and at night in 12 locations in its region. It has developed cooperative programs with various corporations and organizations in the area, designed to prepare skilled workers and upgrade the talents of others. Daker has also taken a leading role in the community in promoting and sponsoring various programs in the arts. It has also attracted large numbers of adults and seniors to credit and noncredit academic and vocational short courses.

Daker Community College is governed by its own board of trustees, an 18-member group of citizens of the region who are appointed by the governor. The board of trustees has the authority to set tuition, construct buildings, establish policy, and appoint the president of the college. Its members represent a cross section of the community and region and accurately reflect the diverse economic and ethnic nature of the area's population. There is a state-wide board of higher education, whose role it is to coordinate the various public universities and community colleges on behalf of the state legislature. However, in recent years, the state-wide board has been ineffective, and the individual colleges and universities in the state have competed with one another for funds in the state legislature.

The president of Daker Community College is Nancy Craig, who was hired by the board of trustees in 2005. She previously served as president of a smaller public community college in another state. She is viewed by her faculty, staff, and others as a strong advocate for her college and, especially, for increased access for all citizens of the state to higher education. Because of the respect she has earned at Daker and the other community colleges in the state, she is often asked to appear before committees in the state legislature when they are considering educational matters.

THE STUDENTS AND THE FACULTY

The students at Daker Community College reflect the diversity of the region of the state where the college is located. About half of the 14,000 students are enrolled in pre-transfer programs, and after these students complete their associate degrees, almost all of them apply to a 4-year institution, where they plan to earn their bachelor's degrees. Although many of the pre-transfer students at Daker continue their studies at the state university in the city, others enroll elsewhere, both within the state and in nearby states. These pre-transfer students at Daker mostly come from within the region, although students can attend the institution from any region of the state. These students are the mostly likely at Daker to be of traditional college age, although almost a fourth of them are 25 years or older. A higher percentage of them are minorities than at any of the state's public universities, and many of them are also first-generation college students.

Because of the great variety of career-oriented students at Daker, it is difficult to describe them as a group. For example, a cohort of 80 students might be enrolled in a computer technician program of 8 months duration, and these students might range in age from 18 to 60. Another program designed to prepare dental assistants might enroll 160 students whose average age is 35. These students often have uneven academic and work backgrounds before they arrive at Daker, and view the institution as providing them with a positive career opportunity in their lives.

The emphasis at Daker is on opportunity and access, and graduates of high schools in the region are admitted to the pre-transfer academic programs at the institution. Students who enter the career-oriented programs have much more varied academic and employment backgrounds; emphasis is not so much on traditional academic credentials as it is on demonstrated competence and individual motivation. A large proportion of Daker Community College students are employed in the area while they are pursuing their degrees or career program certificates; thus, traditional measures of retention are not useful. Many students are enrolled for one term or two and then decide to delay their studies for a while, usually for financial reasons. A majority do return and complete whatever program they had chosen. Many of the students at Daker require compensatory academic training before entering degree programs, as their previous academic work in high school was inadequate or was completed several years ago. Daker is well known for its supportive, individually tailored developmental academic programs in mathematics, reading, and writing, which have provided needed assistance to beginning students for many years.

Student life at Daker is different than at traditional, 4-year universities, where most of the students are full time and reside on campus. At Daker, the campus is busy from 7:00 a.m. until 10:00 p.m., with students mainly attending class. Parking lots encircle the campus, and the students typically drive to campus, go to class, and then leave again, most often to return to their jobs in the city. Despite being a commuter campus with mostly part-time students who live busy lives, there are many student organizations at Daker, representing the varied interests among the student body. The most popular activities center around social events, especially those for students and their families. Student groups that focus on service to the community and outdoor recreation are also popular. There are several sports teams at Daker, and they compete against other community colleges in the state. The most popular of these college teams are men's baseball and women's basketball.

Most students are grateful toward Daker because it represents opportunity to them. This is especially the case for students who were not highly motivated during their earlier years by traditional academic work but now, at another time in their lives, have matured and are eager to learn. Students who have completed various pre-transfer and career-oriented programs at Daker are proud of their accomplishments, and the annual graduation exercises at the institution are not only well attended but are an occasion for heartfelt celebration in the community.

The board of trustees at Daker has worked diligently for many years to make attending Daker affordable to its students. Tuition is low, especially in relation to what students pay at the state universities. Moreover, tuition is charged by credit hour or specific career-oriented program, so students only pay for the courses in which they are enrolled at the time. More than half of the students are enrolled on a part-time basis due to their work schedules and often demanding family responsibilities. Many of the younger, traditional age students live at home and commute to the campus, which is the only way many of the students can afford to attend the institution. Good financial aid programs are available, and many Daker students are recipients of grants, loans, and work-study programs, almost all of which come from the state and federal governments.

The teaching staff at Daker Community College consist of full-time, traditional faculty in basic undergraduate academic disciplines; part-time adjunct faculty who contract to teach only one or two courses for a semester; and working professionals and skilled technicians in the community who teach a night course for a semester. It is difficult to include all the faculty at Daker in one description! Most of them are part time, but almost all of them feel a strong commitment to the institution and are happy to teach there. An engineer at a highly technical manufacturing firm located in the city may teach a course at Daker closely related to his professional expertise, and a full-time biology faculty member may teach traditional undergraduates who intend to transfer to a 4-year university after completing their associate's degree program at Daker. Both are members of the faculty, and both are there because of their love of teaching and their dedication to Daker as an open, caring, and accessible institution.

The faculty at Daker Community College, especially those who are full time, are very involved in the institution, and communications between faculty and administrators are open and frank. Many of the academic and service-oriented innovations at the college are the direct result of suggestions from faculty, and it is common for committees and task forces to be formed among faculty to study various issues and to submit recommendations to the administration for action. The faculty are also engaged with the community, and when new or revised programs are being considered, it is the usual practce to involve well-informed and concerned members of the city and region in discussions and debate.

Although those who teach at Daker are proud of the institution, many of them are frustrated by their salaries, which are considerably lower than their counterparts at the state's public universities. In the earliest years of the institution, both students and faculty were often considered "second class" by the established 4-year institutions, but this view seems to have dissipated in recent years.

There is a Daker Community College Council, which used to be composed only of faculty, but in 2010 includes faculty, staff, students, community leaders, and administrators. Its purpose is to serve as a forum for the discussion of issues of concern to the institution. It meets twice per semester and is chaired by the provost. It does not spend its time considering relatively minor changes in existing academic programs or policies, because these are left to one of its main subgroups, the committee on academic affairs. The Council's role in the work of Daker is important, and President Craig respects its recommendations.

THE ISSUE TO BE ADDRESSED IN THIS CASE STUDY

The legislature has been active in the higher education system of this state for several decades and is frequently lobbied by the presidents of the universities and the community colleges. Per-student funding for public higher education in the state is about average in the country, but tuition for undergraduate students is in the lower third for publicly supported institutions in the United States. The presidents of the two largest public universities in the state have had the support of their boards of trustees for several years to raise tuition to at least the national average for similar institutions, but their efforts have been rejected by the legislature. Tuition for students attending the various community colleges in the state is less than half of what students at the universities pay.

The higher education committee in the state legislature, facing pressure from the voters on a number of issues since the recession of 2008, is not interested in new taxes or any tuition increases at the universities and community colleges. Moreover, the higher education committee and other legislators are hearing criticism from growing numbers of their constituents who are frustrated with the serious shortage of public school teachers, nurses, and other health care professionals in the state. The committee has admonished the state universities to produce more graduates in these fields and has grown angry and impatient with the apparent inability of the universities to do so in recent years. The universities respond to the legislative committee by saying that they have limited resources, that their nursing programs are filled to capacity already, and that decreasing numbers of students are interested in careers as teachers.

The committee held hearings during the legislative session to provide an opportunity to debate these matters and to hear various ideas about how to solve the shortage problems. Various presidents of the universities and of the community colleges were called to appear before the committee, as were representatives of the public school system, the teachers and nurses unions, and other citizen groups. After almost 5 weeks of discussion, no concrete plan emerged from the committee.

The higher education committee then invited a consultant from another state to advise it about ways to address the shortage problem effectively. The consultant suggested permitting the state's community colleges to grant bachelor's degrees in teaching, nursing, and selected health-related fields. The consultant advised that this might open up these fields to more students, and it would also cost less for the state to educate these students in the community colleges. The committee reacted favorably to this idea and announced to the public that it would be holding hearings on the idea beginning the next week. This announcement stunned educators in the state, as if such a measure were adopted, it could result in fundamental changes to both the universities and community colleges.

Almost immediately, the debate became very public, and newspapers, television stations, and blogs carried stories about the "4-year proposal" daily. Those who opposed the idea were quickly labeled elitist or reactionary, and those in favor of it were accused of abandoning the mission of the community college or of being power hungry for expanded programs. Questions were raised and debated about the academic quality of 4-year degrees at the community colleges and about whether such programs could be granted accreditation by the regional accreditation agency. Some also questioned whether students could be convinced to enroll in such untested programs and whether their degrees would enable them to compete successfully with graduates from more traditional bachelor's degree institutions. The presidents of the public universities, most of whom had publicly been supportive of the community colleges for years, found themselves faced with additional competition for students and argued that it would be unfair for the state to grant degrees to students at a much lower cost than what students have to pay at their universities. The community college presidents, who had fought to gain acceptance and credibility for their 2-year academic programs for years, now understood that if they were to include 4-year degrees in their institutions, a similar and perhaps more daunting battle would have to be fought.

After another month of hearings, the state higher education committee voted in favor of the proposal to give the community colleges the authority to grant 4-year degrees in selected fields beginning in 2011. The bill was forwarded to the state house and senate and, after more debate, was passed by a large margin. The governor signed the bill, and it became law.

Nancy Craig, the president of Daker Community College, now has the responsibility of leading her institution's response to this important legislation. She is a long-time advocate for the role of the community college as the most democratic expression of increased educational opportunity in the society. She is also a strong leader who understands and works effectively with the many constituents she knows do not agree with one another on this matter. In considering this issue, the following are some of the options that President Craig may consider.

SOME OPTIONS FOR ADDRESSING THIS ISSUE

1. Urge the legislature and state-wide board of higher education to appoint a special, state-wide task force of community college presidents and state university presidents to study the issue and develop a plan for implementing bachelor's degrees at the community colleges.

President Craig is a respected leader in the state's higher education community, and she is confident that her suggestion will be accepted by legislative officials and the state-wide board of higher education. She believes such a task force is needed to ensure a coordinated approach between the state universities and the community colleges. She is concerned that, without such a coordinated approach, each of the community colleges might develop its own plan and pay little attention to needed communication with the state universities. She believes establishing bachelor's degree programs at the community colleges will require careful planning and open communication to earn acceptance and credibility with the public and with prospective students. She also thinks this approach will make it more likely that the regional accreditation association can be kept well informed and can serve in an advisory role to the task force. President Craig knows the task force should involve professional associations, faculty, and practicing teachers, nurses, and health care providers in the discussion before developing its final recommendations. In this option, Craig feels having the state-wide task force will permit this process to proceed in an orderly and rational manner, making it more likely that the new bachelor's degree programs at the community college might receive public acceptance.

By suggesting this state-wide task force, President Craig may be criticized by some of her colleagues in the community colleges for delaying the opportunity to establish new bachelor's degree programs. This may be the case at Daker Community College, her own institution, as well. Her critics may view her action as risky because they feel this is a great opportunity and worry that the state universities are not in favor of it and will certainly lobby to repeal the legislative action during the next year. By including the state university presidents on the task force, President Craig hopes to ensure their cooperation, but of course just the opposite might happen. Privately, she would like to move ahead and implement bachelor's degree programs in teacher education, nursing, and health-related professions on her own campus right away. However, she feels if she did so without cooperation and collaboration with the other community colleges and state universities, she would be subject to public criticism, and, worse, the new degree programs might not succeed as a result. She is aware that the state university presidents do not like the bill and will try to prevent the community colleges from offering bachelor's degrees. However, she also knows that many members of the public are frustrated with the high costs of attending the state universities, and the legislature is not satisfied with the shortages of teachers, nurses, and health care providers. Thus, she knows that any public argument made by the state university presidents to block this bill will be difficult to sustain.

2. Refer the matter to the Daker Community College Council and ask for the Council's evaluation of the legislation and whether Daker should establish the bachelor's degree programs on its campus.

President Craig knows well her college and its traditions for involving faculty and staff in policy, curriculum, and program decisions. She knows it would be a mistake for her to move to adopt the new program or to reject it without a genuine and open consideration of its advantages and disadvantages for the institution. Without the active involvement of the Daker Community College Council, she feels any decision about this important program would have little chance of success. To make it work, the faculty, in particular, need to be committed to it and to carefully consider how to implement the significant changes required. She also knows that if this plan, or even part of it, is implemented, there will be increased costs involved, and that additional faculty will have to be hired. Thus, she insists that her senior financial officer will be part of the Council's deliberations and eventual recommendation to her. Before referring this matter to the Council, of course, President Craig explains her plan of action to the board of trustees and gains its approval. She also carefully assesses what her presidential colleagues in the other community colleges may choose to do; she wants to cooperate with them, but she also wants Daker Community College to be viewed as a leader in this new venture and does not want to be the last community college in the state to act on this matter. In referring this issue to the Council, President Craig is affirming the important role it has in Daker's decision-making process and expressing her confidence in it. She feels this is a necessary step and wants to move forward. Thus, she gives the Council only 4 months to review and consider the issue and present her with its recommendations.

In this option, President Craig may be criticized for not moving fast enough by those who view the new bachelor's degree programs as a great opportunity for Daker Community College. These critics feel Daker may be left behind by the other community colleges if it does not act right away. Craig is privately hopeful that the Council will decide that the new degree programs are a good idea and recommend that they should be implemented. However, by asking the Council for its evaluation of the legislation and whether Daker should establish the new degree programs, she obviously runs the risk of getting a negative review from the Council. Although she knows this can happen, she thinks it is unlikely but admits to herself that if it does happen, it will be difficult to move in another direction. If the Council rejects the idea of the new degree programs and some of the other community colleges move ahead with them, she knows many outside of her college will wonder why Daker is not offering these new degrees. Finally, President Craig knows this is one of the most important issues her college has ever faced—one that could change the nature of the institution, and she wants to be thorough in evaluating all aspects of the program before moving ahead with it.

3. Seize the opportunity the state legislature has provided and move ahead as soon as possible to implement the new bachelor's degree programs at Daker Community College.

President Daker is a strong leader, and she is excited about the opportunity to establish bachelor's degree programs at Daker. She views it as a transforming change at her institution, and she feels it is her responsibility to implement these new programs as quickly as she can. She knows the politics of this situation in her state are complicated, and she is convinced that the state universities and their supporters will lobby to get this legislation repealed soon. She believes that Daker can do an excellent job of providing bachelor's degree programs in teaching, nursing, and health-related professions, and she and her provost already have carefully considered what resources are needed. She also will collaborate with faculty at the state university located in the same city as

Daker on the best ways to implement these degree programs. She knows that some of the university faculty may not be supportive of her plans to proceed, but if she can gain the cooperation and participation of some of them, she knows it will strengthen the programs and also diminish some of the objections from them. She is confident that she can convince her own board of trustees that moving ahead with the new bachelor's degree programs is the right thing to do and that it is important to do it now. Privately, she is determined that Daker will be the first community college in the state to implement the new degree programs, because this will confirm the institution's reputation for innovation and responsiveness to the public. She has already met with her admissions and financial aid staff and feels that Daker can attract students who will want to complete their bachelor's degrees at the institution. President Craig likes leading an institution that is viewed as a pioneer in its academic programs, and she feels that these new bachelor's degree programs present her and Daker with a great opportunity.

In this option, President Craig is assuming the role of a forceful leader. She may involve the college council in some discussions but only to help her implement the new degree programs, not to debate whether the college should accept the idea! She feels obligated to act as quickly as she can, although she knows some faculty and staff will question whether her action is wise in the long run for the college. Her critics may accuse her of being overly directive and of not being loyal to the traditional role of the community college. She knows she must be active and persuasive about what she wants to do with this program, and she also must be willing to accept the inevitable criticism from those who oppose it. But she knows she has the support of her board of trustees, and she also believes the state legislature may be more apt to allocate additional funds to her college if and when she implements the program they have just passed! In response to her faculty critics who ask how the other academic programs at Daker will be affected by this change, Craig assures them that the college will continue to offer all of the same programs it has in the past; these new programs are, in fact, merely extensions of academic programs already in place at the college. Finally, she argues that this may be a once-in-a-lifetime opportunity for the college to expand its impact and its service to the people and that Daker should take full advantage of it.

4. Reject the idea of establishing bachelor's degree programs at Daker, arguing that this is inconsistent with the idea of a community college.

President Craig, after discussing this issue with her board and trustees and the Daker Community College Council, decides not to participate in it and rejects the idea as being fundamentally inconsistent with the major purposes of a community college. Craig has spent her entire career in community colleges as a faculty member, dean, provost, and president, and she believes these colleges have an important and unique niche in higher education, which is to serve the educational and career needs of the public. She feels that moving her institution to include bachelor's degrees would change the focus away from the academic and career needs of students not served by 4-year colleges and universities. She thinks that it would only be a matter of time that the emphasis and financial resources would be shifted to these 4-year programs and that the traditional career and pre-transfer programs would become a lower priority. She also resents what she considers the major motivation by the legislature in passing this bill, which is to produce more teachers, nurses, and health-related providers for less money. She believes this will cause the public to think these bachelors degrees earned at her college will inevitably be viewed as second rate by the public. She is intensely proud of the academic excellence of the programs in place at Daker now and does not want to compromise their reputation by shifting resources to 4-year degree programs. She is aware that other community colleges in the state may choose another direction, but she wants to maintain the integrity of Daker Community College by continuing its commitment to its educational mission of addressing the needs of the entire community. While rejecting the idea now, President Craig leaves open the possibility she and her college may revisit it sometime in the future.

Sometimes it takes more courage as an academic leader to decline an opportunity to expand programs than it takes to accept and implement them. President Craig knows she is making a decision on this issue, which might confuse and even anger the legislators who passed this bill, but she feels it is the right decision and is consistent with the role and purpose of her institution. She will try to help these legislators understand her position. She does not deny that there is a shortage of teachers, nurses, and health-related providers in the state, but she does resent that the legislature expects the community colleges to solve the problem and to do so with less money. She thinks the legislature is letting the state universities off the hook for not producing enough graduates in these needed areas and is merely dumping its problem on the community colleges. As a principled academic leader, she is not so naïve as to jump at this bait! She suspects that some of her colleagues at the other state community colleges are willing to implement the bachelor's degree programs primarily because they think that, by doing so, their academic prestige will be elevated. She disagrees with this view and feels it is her responsibility as president of Daker to reject the idea of establishing bachelor's degree programs at her institution and explain her reasons to the public.

QUESTIONS THAT MAY AID IN THE DISCUSSION OF THIS CASE STUDY

1. Can President Craig really "go her own way" on this matter, rejecting the opportunity to implement the new programs, especially if the other community colleges in the state do accept it?
2. If additional financial support from the state is not allocated to Daker for these new bachelor's degree programs, it will obviously require some significant revisions in its internal budget. If this is the case, should Daker decide to move ahead with the programs anyway?
3. If the new bachelor's programs are accepted, how can their academic credibility be established? Should Daker simply duplicate what the state universities are doing in their bachelor's degree programs in teacher education, nursing, and health-related professions or should it try to do something new?
4. Should higher tuition be charged to the students who enroll in the new bachelor's degree programs at Daker?

Suggested Readings Related to This Case

Floyd, Deborah L., Skolnik, Michael L., & Walker, Kenneth P. (2006). *The Community College Baccalaureate: Emerging Trends and Policy Issues.* Sterling, VA: Stylus Publishing.

Kezar, Adrianna. (2001). *Understanding and Facilitating Change in Higher Education in the 21st Century.* San Francisco: Jossey Bass.

Roueche, John E., Richardson, M. Melissa, Neal, Philip W., & Roueche, Suanne D. (2008). *The Creative Community College: Leading Change Through Innovation.* Washington, DC: Community College Press/American Association of Community Colleges.

Weisman, Iris M., & Vaughan, George B. (1997). *Presidents and Trustees in Partnership: New Roles and Leadership Challeges. New Directions for Community Colleges.* San Francisco: Jossey Bass.

Chapter 4

CASE STUDIES IV:
STUDENT SERVICES ISSUES

A STUDENT PROTEST AT KELLSTROME COLLEGE

RETHINKING A STATE MERIT-BASED SCHOLARSHIP
    PROGRAM

ADDRESSING ALCOHOL ABUSE AT HENKEL COLLEGE

EVALUATING THE PERFORMANCE OF THE DEAN OF
    STUDENTS AT CABRERA COLLEGE

RESTRUCTURING CAREER SERVICES AT CLAIRE STATE
    UNIVERSITY

A STUDENT PROTEST AT
KELLSTROME COLLEGE

SUMMARY OF THE CASE

Kellstrome College is a private institution located in the Southeastern United States. Its enrollment is 3,600 students, all of whom are undergraduates. In the past 20 years, Kellstrome has worked to increase the number of African-American students on the campus. The college believes in the educational value of a diverse student body, which is consistent with its stated mission of "education for service to others." Kellstrome is affiliated with the Quaker tradition. Of the 3,600 students currently enrolled at the college, 380 are African American. This represents a significant increase, as only 20 years ago, the total number of African-American students at Kellstrome was only 50. In 1990, a new president was hired by the board of trustees, and she led the college to actively recruit more African-American students. In 2010, almost everyone associated with the college believes it was the right thing to do and that it has helped to improve the quality of the educational experience at the institution. As a private college with a modest endowment, Kellstrome is dependent on tuition income, and its costs are $41,000 per year, about average for residential private institutions in its area in 2010. The college has provided substantial institutional aid to its African-American students, but now, with the recession of 2008 making its impact, many of these students object to another increase in tuition at Kellstrome, saying they simply cannot afford to remain at the college. After expressing their feelings to faculty, financial aid staff, and the dean of student affairs, they are frustrated when they receive no assurance of help, and about 100 of them decide to move into the president's office in the administration building, saying they will not leave until the college promises them more

164

financial aid. This sit-in continued, gained more momentum and support from other students, and received extensive press coverage. The students say they will not leave, and the dean of student affairs is struggling to decide how to resolve the situation.

A DESCRIPTION OF KELLSTROME COLLEGE

Kellstrome College, named after the small town in which it is located, was founded by a group of Quakers in 1912 to provide higher education to young people with a strong emphasis on the values of peace, love, and service to others. Their objective was to prepare educated young people for a life of service to others regardless of the field of study they were pursuing. The college remained small for many years, and only survived, especially during the Great Depression, because of the financial support of many committed donors and the willingness of the faculty to accept low salaries. But after World War II the college began to grow, and its commitment to service and caring campus culture became attractive to many young students. When its enrollment reached 3,600 in 1978, the board of trustees decided this was the maximum number of students it felt could be accommodated effectively to achieve its educational mission.

The college has extensive academic offerings, but all students complete a strong general education core of courses in the humanities, social science, biological science, and physical science. In all of their academic work, students are encouraged by faculty to seek connections to the idea of service to others. All students are required to participate in a one-semester "service experience" in a needy community in either the United States or abroad. These semester experiences are a highlight of the students' undergraduate years and are closely supervised by faculty advisers.

Kellstrome College is governed by a board of trustees, which consists of almost 50 professional, business, and community leaders mainly from the state and region. A group of 10 of these trustees serves as the executive board and oversees the affairs of the college more closely than the full board, which meets only once per year. The president of Kellstrome is Helen Osborne, who has been in her position for 20 years. She is considered among the top private college presidents in the country and is often in demand as a speaker and consultant to other educational institutions. She is respected at Kellstrome, although she is not well known to most students.

The dean of student affairs at Kellstrome is Roger Hunt, who was hired by President Osborne in 2003. He previously served as a professor of history at Kellstrome and was selected to be the dean because of his strong commitment to the educational and service goals of the college and his excellent relationships with students. As the dean of student affairs, Hunt has administrative responsibility for admissions, financial aid, housing, and the other student services at Kellstrome.

Kellstrome has a modest endowment of $300 million. It has increased since President Osborne came to the college due largely to her leadership and direct involvement in development activities. But she and her colleagues recognize that the endowment needs to grow, especially in view of the increasing cost to attend the college and the college's determination to maintain a diverse student body. The great majority of the 380 African-American students at Kellstrome come from low- to middle-income families, and the college is struggling to provide adequate financial aid to these students to keep them at the institution. The president and board of trustees do not want to see Kellstrome become a college that only students from affluent families can attend. The endowment's value has decreased since the recession of 2008, making it difficult for the college to assist students with more financial aid.

THE STUDENTS AND THE FACULTY

The students at Kellstrome mainly come from within the state and region. Most of them were in the top one third of their high school classes. Admission to Kellstrome is not highly competitive, and well over half of the students who apply are accepted. Most students are attracted to Kellstrome either because their families have a connection to the institution or they share the values for which the college is known. Most of the students have already been quite involved in community and social service activities before they enroll at Kellstrome, and they expect to continue in these activities while in college.

Student life at Kellstrome is active, with students engaged in social and recreational programs. The college is located in a beautiful area, with woods, lakes, streams, and small mountains, making the environment ideal for outdoor activities. Most of the students live on campus in college residence halls, and there are more than 100 student groups at Kellstrome, reflecting the varied interests of the student body.

Student groups at Kellstrome have traditionally been conservative in style but active in their interest in social issues, especially those affecting poor and disadvantaged people. When there are problems facing communities in the area due to floods or storms, Kellstrome student groups are usually among the first to be there offering help to others.

There is a student government association at the college, and it coordinates the activities of the many student organizations. It administers a student activity fee in support of various functions on the campus. It also serves as the representative of the student body at the Kellstrome Community Council. This council, composed of students, faculty, and staff, is very important at the college. It represents the values of the college and its belief that issues and problems should be considered in a peaceful, open, and respectful manner. It meets once per month, and it is the place at Kellstrome where anyone can go to be heard and where issues of concern to the academic community are considered. It has no formal power to make policy, but it is influential, and administrators at the college pay close attention to its deliberations. Although less than half of the students and faculty at the college are Quakers, this model of the "Quaker meeting" is a highly respected tradition at Kellstrome and an important part of its culture.

Most of the students become quite attached to the college, and few of them leave before graduation or transfer to other institutions. At graduation, many of them accept jobs in social service agencies, nonprofit organizations, and schools. However, in recent years, the most popular academic major is business, and more and more students are seeking jobs in corporations. Almost 20 percent of students graduating from Kellstrome enter graduate or professional school.

The "service experience" semester is an important part of the educational program at Kellstrome. With the advice and guidance from their faculty advisers, students spend a semester with a community service agency in the United States or in another country. This represents a major commitment by the college to its values of service to others. The students' experiences are closely monitored by faculty members, and students are required to submit a major paper on their experience and also make a presentation at a seminar in their academic department when they return. This one-semester service experience is often described by students as the most important and valuable one in their years at the college.

In the past 20 years, the enrollment of African-American students at Kellstrome has increased from 50 to 380. The college has worked hard to ensure that these students become part of the traditions at Kellstrome. Most of the African-American students enrolled at the college because they were also attracted to Kellstrome's commitment to service to others. For many of them, adjusting to the predominantly white college has been difficult, and although most of them find the college community to be friendly and supportive, others have felt lonely. Because most of the African-American students at Kellstrome come from low- to middle-income families, paying for the high costs of attendance has been almost a constant concern for them.

The faculty at Kellstrome College are more diverse than they were 25 years ago. In 2010, fewer of them come from Quaker beginnings, but nevertheless they are committed to the special values of the college and the philosophy of service to others. Because there are no graduate programs at Kellstrome, the faculty are primarily engaged in teaching, and they also serve as involved advisers to students. Faculty not only know the names of their students, they often have met their families and know a good deal about their students' interests and what they intend to do with their lives after graduation.

Students who expect to be left alone in college or to have complete independence most likely would do better not to attend Kellstrome! Early in their freshman year, the students begin regular meetings with their faculty adviser, and the same adviser remains assigned to the student until graduation unless the student requests a change. Most academic departments have various social and service-related events throughout the year, and students and faculty participate with each other on intramural recreational sports teams.

Almost all of the faculty at Kellstrome have the academic credentials to work at more research-oriented universities, but they have chosen to teach at Kellstrome. They enjoy the informal, friendly, and open culture at the college and in the community as well. They are proud of the college's high academic standards and, especially, of its serious commitment to its values of civility, fairness, and service to others. Most of them genuinely enjoy being at Kellstrome, and, once part of the college, most stay until retirement.

There are several academic departments at the college, but the institution works hard to create unity and coherence in what the students study. The strong general education requirements essentially ensure that the students will share many similar intellectual experiences during their 4 years at Kellstrome. But in recent years, students have expressed more interest in a specific academic major, making it more difficult for the college to sustain its broad liberal arts emphasis for all students.

Faculty are active participants in the decision-making process at Kellstrome, and they do this primarily through the Kellstrome Community Council. In the Quaker tradition, everyone is encouraged to become part of the deliberations, and respect for the opinions of others is an honored tradition. However, discussions of campus issues, especially those concerning the curriculum, can become lively at the Council, and on some occasions more than 200 students, faculty, and staff will be part of these meetings. The distance between faculty and administrators at Kellstrome is not as great as it is at most other institutions, and the tradition of collegiality and trust remains high.

THE ISSUE TO BE ADDRESSED IN THIS CASE STUDY

Roger Hunt, the dean of student affairs at Kellstrome, is in charge of the admissions and financial aid offices and has been the primary administrator charged with the responsibility for recruiting and retaining African-American students. He has been in his position since 2003 and was a faculty member for several years before being appointed the dean. He is well known on this small campus and loves spending time with students. He is strongly committed to the values of the college and is respected for his hard work, honesty, and expertise in admissions and financial aid.

He was hired by President Osborne partly because of his strong commitment to recruiting African-American students to Kellstrome. He and the president are well aware that the college has had to use significant dollars from its endowment to provide needed financial aid to these students and other Kellstrome students who come from poor families. The financial aid office has been aggressive and successful in securing state and federal funds for students with need, but to attract and retain students from low-income families, these funds are insufficient. Institutional funds must make up the difference, and with a relatively small (and decreasing!) college endowment, Roger Hunt knows he and the institution are facing a serious problem.

Hunt and the staff in admissions and financial aid have reached out to African-American students who come from lower income families and have tried to make adjustments in their financial aid packages that will enable them to remain at Kellstrome. But this is becoming more difficult each year, especially since the recession of 2008, as many of the students' parents lost their jobs. For the fall of 2010, the number of African-American freshmen who began their studies at Kellstrome dropped by 50 percent—a direct result of insufficient institutional financial aid available for them. Equally of concern to Hunt and his staff is that 35 African-American sophomores and juniors at the college decided to leave the institution and transfer to less expensive public colleges close to home. These students indicated to Hunt and his staff that they greatly regretted having to leave Kellstrome, but they and their families simply could no longer afford to stay.

Hunt and his staff have made special efforts to stay in touch with the most needy African-American students, but they know that these students are frustrated with their financial problems and that this level of frustration is growing. Nevertheless, Hunt and others were stunned when a group of about 100 African-American students decided to walk into President Osborne's office in the administration building and announce that they were not leaving until their demands for financial aid were met. Such an action was unprecedented at Kellstrome and was viewed as a direct contradiction of the values of trust, openness, and collegiality that the college teaches.

The group of students was polite to the administrators and other staff in the building but informed them they they did not plan to leave until their demands were met. They presented the president's assistant (Osborne was out of town) with a written list of their concerns, some of which further surprised Dean Hunt, his staff, and others. Besides demanding sufficient financial aid to enable them to remain at the college, the student group also listed the following demands: (1) the hiring of more African-American faculty at Kellstrome, (2) a special house or meeting space devoted to the African-American student association, and (3) the ending of what they term hostile treatment in the residence halls from white students.

Dean Hunt went to the administration building to ensure that the students were safe. During this time, Hunt and his staff continued to converse with the students. After the sit-in began, it quickly became known on this small campus, and about 50 other students joined the sit-in to indicate their support for the demands presented by the African-American students. Even in this small community, this action attracted the press, and students participating in the sit-in watched themselves on the television news that night. Most people at Kellstrome were surprised upon learning of the sit-in and wondered how such an event could happen at the college.

Dean Hunt knows it is his responsibility to try to resolve this crisis at Kellstrome College. The following are some of the options he is considering:

SOME OPTIONS FOR ADDRESSING THIS ISSUE

1. Inform the student protesters that they are in violation of the law and of Kellstrome College rules, that they have 30 minutes to leave the building, or they will be removed and arrested for trespassing.

Dean Hunt knows almost all of the students participating in the sit-in, but his personal efforts to reason with them are rebuffed. After about 2 hours, he decides to have the students removed. He is angry with the students for violating not only the college rules, but for resorting to a method that contradicts the trust, respect, and collegiality so valued by Kellstrome College. He understands the financial frustrations the protesting students are facing, but he does not condone their method of protesting. He tells the students that decisions at the college can never be made via threat or intimidation and that they will be held accountable for their violation of college rules. Because Kellstrome has such a small police force, Hunt contacts the city police, who come to the campus. After being warned that they are breaking the law and will be arrested if they do not leave, the protesting students remain in the president's office. However, when the police move in to the office, the students allow themselves to be arrested in a peaceful manner and leave the building. After being taken to the police station in busses and formally charged with trespassing, the students are released and return to the campus. The students are tired and return to their residence halls for the night. The next day, they receive a letter from Dean Hunt inform-

ing them they will each have to appear before the campus judicial officer because of their violation of the campus rule against disrupting campus offices and activities.

In taking this action, Dean Hunt is sending a message that law and rule breaking at Kellstrome is unacceptable, that it is inconsistent with the values of the college, and that there will be consequences for the students' actions. He will be applauded by those who believe that such actions by students cannot be tolerated and criticized by others who think his actions are authoritarian and overly harsh. Hunt is well aware that his decision to remove the students will be questioned at the college and in the community, but he is willing to live with the criticism. He is confident in the support of his president, Helen Osborne, who was out of town during the sit-in but was kept informed of the situation by Dean Hunt. He is fully aware that simply having the students removed from the president's office will not do anything to resolve their grievances, especially their personal financial problems. He is shaken by the students' demands for more African-American faculty, a meeting house, and especially, their feelings of being treated in a hostile manner by their fellow students in the residence halls. He fears that the issues may now be even more challenging to deal with after he has had the students forcibly removed from the administration building, but he does not regret doing so, because he does not believe such actions are justified or necessary in bringing about change at the college. He must now work to bring the college community together for open discussion of the problems raised by the student protesters, try to heal some of the pain felt by students and faculty, and seek a resolution to these difficult issues.

2. Have the students removed from the building but grant Dean Hunt the authority to negotiate with them to resolve the issue.

Dean Hunt understands the problems that the African-American students at the college are facing, and he feels that there has been enough conversation and discussion about these issues. He also does not want the college to lose these students or not to live up to its obligations to support them. Especially after his decision to have the protesting students removed from the administration building, he also senses that this situation could easily and quickly escalate into a much worse set of problems for the college and its students. He feels the matters should be addressed directly now and that he should have the authority to nego- tiate a solution with the affected students. After some conversation with President Osborne and the chair of the board of trustees, Hunt is given assur- ance that adequate funds will be made available for him to support the cur- rently enrolled students' financial needs. Although he recognizes that this approach is not the usual way of resolving problems at Kellstrome, he feels the situation is so volatile that it needs to be settled now. He is confident in his ability to secure the students' support at least on the matter of their financial needs. He will assure the students that their other grievances will be carefully considered. He recognizes that the board of trustees has made a substantial financial commitment to these students but that he also cannot make any promises for newly recruited African-American students to the college at this time. Thus, Hunt decides to negotiate with the students and resolve the finan- cial issues they are facing by providing them with special grants from the board of trustees.

In this option, Dean Hunt is relying on the confidence his president and board of trustees have in him to solve this problem before it gets even uglier for the college. Because he has earned the respect of the Kellstrome College community for his hard work, honesty, and con- cern for students for several years, his judgment in this matter is trust- ed by his president and board. He does not like this model of decision making and feels that the student sit-in represents a failure on his part and on the part of the college. The college initiated the recruitment program many years ago and should have anticipated the real prob- lems the students would face in a more realistic and sensitive manner. Hunt is proud of what many of these African-American students have accomplished at the college, what they have contributed to the cam- pus, and what they will do in the future. He does not want to lose any of this and is willing to take this unusual action to support the students. If he is successful in resolving the financial situation of the current stu- dents, he will still hold them accountable for the violation of college rules when they sat in the president's office, but he knows the sanc- tions will be quite mild. He strongly suspects that the trespassing charges for the students will eventually be dropped by the city. He knows he and his staff have a lot of work to do to restore trust with the students and to resolve the other grievances they have presented. Finally, Hunt is well aware that he will be criticized by some at the college for "rewarding the students' inappropriate behavior" by granting them the money they need.

3. Do not remove the students from the building and involve faculty and student leaders in open conversation and debate about the issues.

Kellstrome College is a special place, and it has its own ways of resolving its problems. These ways have always reflected the core values of the college: trust, peace, and respect for others. Although the sit-in is unprecedented at the college and shocked most students and faculty, almost everyone at the college recognizes that it would be a mistake to ignore the student protesters and show disdain for them by not listening carefully to what they want to say. Moreover, the traditions at the college for dealing with issues have to do with talking, listening, and compromise. This is a trusting community, and there is no immediate need to force the protesting students from the administration building. Thus, in this option, Dean Hunt exhorts his fellow students and faculty at the college to come to the administration building and engage in peaceful and caring discussion with the student protesters. As a matter of fact, he asks them to bring food and drinks for the student protesters and any academic materials they may need to keep up with their class work. He has assured others (including the president) that no damage will be done to her office or to the building, and he has arranged for no police officers to be present. He is not particularly worried about how long the student protesters intend to stay in the building; he is confident that a large demonstration of caring concern by the Kellstrome community will assure the student protesters that their issues are being heard, that the traditions of respect and peace are in place, and that they are valued members of the college community. Hunt has great faith in the power of the Kellstrome community to help resolve the issues the student protesters have raised, and he is confident that this option has the best chance of success in the long run. He also views it as an ideal "teaching moment" for the students to learn about how the values of Kellstrome College can serve as a model for resolving problems.

Dean Hunt is not so naïve that he thinks the financial and other issues the protesting students have presented will be completely resolved by many hours (or even 3 days!) of informal discussion in the hallways and offices of the administration building. But he believes this approach is necessary to allow the student concerns to be heard and to engage many others in the college in the issues. He is under no great pressure by his president or the board of trustees to have the students removed, and he is optimistic that in time the students will decide to leave the building peaceably after becoming convinced that the college community is listening to their concerns and will move ahead in sincere efforts to resolve them. Hunt was a participant in "teach-ins" during the 1960s as a graduate student at a large public university. He believes much more positive results can emerge from a campus sit-in by meeting with the students and listening to them, as opposed to forcibly removing students and inevitably polarizing the issues by such action. During the informal conversations at the sit-in sight, Hunt must have confidence that what he says to the student protesters will be supported by President Osborne and the board of trustees. He must also rely on the trust and respect he has developed over the past few years with faculty and student leaders. He knows their participation and willingness to listen and offer alternatives to the student protesters will go a long way in helping to defuse the situation. Finally, Hunt knows that his future as dean of student affairs at Kellstrome probably will be decided by how well this option works out.

4. Convince the students to leave the administration building, assure them that no disciplinary action will be taken against them, and refer the entire matter to the Kellstrome College Community Council to be considered and resolved.

In this option, Dean Hunt meets with the student protesters in the administration building and, after a lengthy but peaceful discussion, assures the students that he has listened carefully to their demands and grievances. He assures them if they leave the building immediately in a peaceful manner, he will refer this matter to the Kellstrome College Community Council to be carefully considered and resolved. To reinforce this move, he informs the student protesters that President Osborne and the chair of the council have agreed to this action. He knows that everyone at the college has great respect for the council, as the embodiment of the values for which Kellstrome stands. Issues considered by the council are given fair treatment, and those members of the college community appearing before it to present their concerns are respected. Moreover, the conclusions reached by the council are the result of open and honest deliberation and are almost always accepted by the president. The council has a positive rep-

utation at the college, and Hunt is confident that the students' grievances will receive a full and fair airing there. However, he knows he must gain assurances from the president and board of trustees about what financial options the council may have before it begins its discussion of the students' grievances and demands. Although Hunt has confidence in the council, he also knows it can take a long time to make decisions and is sometimes so sincere in wanting to hear all sides of every issue that it may frustrate those impatient for action. In his private meetings with council members, he plans on urging them to move ahead with this matter, because he is worried that if the students see no action for too long, the situation will get worse.

In this option, Dean Hunt is relying on the trusted Community Council to defuse the situation and assure the students that their issues will be fairly considered by the college. He knows this cannot work unless the students trust him and the council. He was pleased that he was able to save the college further public embarrassment by convincing the students to leave the administration building in a peaceable manner, but he is anxious about how cordial some council members will be to the students after their unprecedented action of conducting the sit-in. He is also concerned about what he knows are some pockets of lingering prejudice toward African Americans among students and faculty at Kellstrome, but he hopes the college's traditional values of acceptance, respect, and love will prevail. He knows as well that, by his actions, he is placing the "burden" of dealing with this issue on the council and is expecting support from the president and the board of trustees as well. If the council is unable to make any progress in satisfying the student demands and grievances, he knows he will have to intervene. Finally, Hunt and his staff must continue to remain in close personal contact with the protesting students because he knows they are under a good deal of strain.

QUESTIONS THAT MAY AID IN THE DISCUSSION OF THIS CASE STUDY

1. If Dean Hunt believes there is little hope that there will be adequate financial resources available in the future for the support of African-American students, how can he, in good faith, negotiate with the student protesters?

2. If President Osborne and the board of trustees insist on Option 1, where the students are arrested and removed right away, and Dean Hunt is strongly opposed to taking such action, should he resign?
3. If Dean Hunt and his staff were really as close to the students as they claim to be, why couldn't they have known about the sit-in beforehand and averted it?
4. Administrative and academic leaders serve at the pleasure of their presidents. Would it be possible for Hunt to pursue any of the options described earlier without the support and approval of his president?

Suggested Readings Related to This Case

Baruch Bush, Robert A., & Folger, Joseph P. (2004). *The Promise of Mediation: The Transformative Approach to Conflict.* San Francisco: Jossey Bass.

Cheldelin, Sandra I. , & Lucas, Ann F. (2003). *Academic Administrator's Guide to Conflict Resolution.* San Francisco: Jossey Bass.

McClinton, Marguerite, & Dalton, Jon C. (2002). *The Art and Practical Wisdom of Student Affairs Leadership.* San Francisco: Jossey Bass.

Meyer, David S. (2006). *The Politics of Protest: Social Movements in America.* New York: Oxford University Press.

RETHINKING A STATE MERIT-BASED SCHOLARSHIP PROGRAM

SUMMARY OF THE CASE

Blanchert State University, a comprehensive, land-grant institution with 32,000 students, is located in the Southwest. It is one of five public universities in its state and is, by far, the most selective of these institutions. In 2004, the state legislature established a merit-based scholarship program for state residents in order to encourage more of the state's most talented high school students to attend its public universities. This merit scholarship is awarded on the basis of high school grades and scores on the SAT and amounts to a maximum of $4,500 per student per year, which is close to the actual undergraduate tuition. The scholarship became very popular and resulted in an increased number of academically talented in-state students at Blanchert State. After 6 years of this program, the state legislature, now faced with the economic recession and rising costs of this merit scholarship, is debating whether the state can afford it any longer and whether it is a wise use of taxpayer funds. A new president has just been appointed at Blanchert State. Because her institution's students are the main beneficiaries of this merit scholarship, she must now make her recommendations about the program to her board of trustees and to the state legislature.

A DESCRIPTION OF BLANCHERT STATE UNIVERSITY

Founded in 1888, Blanchert State University has grown to become a large, research-oriented, land-grant institution. It enrolls 32,000 students, including 5,200 in its various graduate programs and three professional schools. It is located in an attractive city of 40,000 residents, and about half of the undergraduate students live on the campus. Only about 10 percent of the undergraduate students come from other states. Its relatively low tuition, good academic reputation, and active student life have made it the most popular and largest university in the state. There are four other public universities in the state, none of which has an enrollment of more than 11,000 students. The only publicly supported professional schools in the state are at Blanchert State.

The university is well known in the Southwest for its programs in medicine, law, pharmacy, business administration, and agriculture. Graduate students come to Blanchert State from most states and from more than 30 foreign countries. There are almost 3,000 international students at the university, and minorities comprise almost 30 percent of the student body, accurately reflecting the racial and ethnic population of the state.

The university has a highly visible intercollegiate athletic program, and its football and basketball games attract thousands of fans and are popular with the students as well. Sports are an important part of the student life of Blanchert State.

The institution, while successful, has been concerned for many years that many of the state's most outstanding high school students have opted not to attend a college or university within the state but have preferred to attend a college or university in another part of the country. Efforts have been made to attract more of these high-achieving students, but for the most part they have not been successful. Blanchert State's reputation among undergraduates has been that it is quite easy to gain admission, its academic requirements have not been overly demanding, and that it is an enjoyable place to attend college.

The university did not have an active fundraising program for many years, and thus its endowment is only about $200 million, among the lowest in the country for large, public land-grant institutions. Blanchert State's new president, Roberta Snyder, intends to make fundraising a high priority, and her previous success in this area as a president of another university made her attractive to the board of trustees. The board has confidence that Snyder will be able to increase the endowment.

Blanchert State University is one of five public universities in the state, each of which has its own board of trustees appointed by the governor of the state. Blanchert State, being the oldest, largest, and most comprehensive of the five institutions, has received the most funding per student from the state legislature for many years. Relationships between the Blanchert State board of trustees and the state legislature have often been strained, and the leaders of the four smaller public universities have complained for many years that their funding is inadequate, especially in comparison with what Blanchert State receives. The four smaller public institutions are not selective in their undergraduate admissions and mainly serve lower to middle- class students in their region of the state. There are eight privately supported colleges in the state, but none is very well known outside of the state, and Blanchert State does not compete with them very often for new undergraduate students.

THE STUDENTS AND THE FACULTY

The undergraduates who attend Blanchert State are mainly residents of the state. Competition to gain admission is not very rigorous, and most students with reasonably good academic records are admitted. Students enjoy their time at the university, and once enrolled most stay until graduation. The university accepts more than 600 transfer students each year, mainly from the other four public colleges in the state. Because of its traditions and greater visibility, Blanchert State is viewed as the most desirable university in the state by most young people.

Student life is traditional and very active, with students involved in hundreds of organizations and activities. There are many campus residence halls and a thriving Greek system, with facilities that house more than 3,000 students. Blanchert State is located in a state known for its conservative politics, and this is reflected in student life. Religious, social, and recreational activities are popular, but there is little political activity among the students. The student government association focuses its attention mainly on campus social activities and rarely expresses its views about university academic policies and programs.

The most popular academic majors for Blanchert State students in recent years are business administration, accounting, education, biology, and psychology. The brightest undergraduates most often appear in engineering and the biological and physical sciences.

Although Blanchert State students are mostly happy to be there, they have known over the years that many of their high-achieving high school friends have chosen to attend various out-of-state colleges, feeling that Blanchert State's academic reputation was not as strong as it could be. Many of the university's students would have chosen to attend college elsewhere but decided to enroll at Blanchert State because of its comparatively low cost, convenient location, and attractive student life.

Most of Blanchert State's students come from middle- to upper middle-income families, and many are sons and daughters of alumni. Many of the students are recipients of state and federal financial aid, most in the form of loans. Little institutional aid is provided given the relatively small endowment. However, the merit scholarship program started by the state legislature in 2004 has grown rapidly, and because it has been relatively easy to meet the academic qualifications set by the state, more than 85 percent of Blanchert State's undergraduates are now recipients of this scholarship! The annual awards average $4,500 per year and cover most of the undergraduate tuition.

Blanchert State is located in a very diverse state, and its minority enrollment is almost 30 percent. However, even with this relatively high percentage, there is considerable criticism of the university for not making greater efforts to increase its minority enrollment and to increase its access to first-generation students from poor families.

The 5,200 graduate students mainly come from other colleges and universities in the Southwest, but in recent years increasing numbers have come from other areas of the country. Graduate students also come to Blanchert State from more than 30 countries, greatly enhancing the diversity of the campus. The provost and graduate dean at the university are aware that the stipends for graduate and research assistantships at Blanchert State are not competitive with those at their peer institutions, but they have not been successful at convincing the state legislature to grant more funds for this purpose. Without a substantial endowment, enhanced financial support to attract more competitive graduate students has been challenging.

Graduate students are focused mainly on their academic programs and have not been active as a group on campus issues for many years. However, with the recession of 2008, the graduate student council was revived and has petitioned the provost and graduate dean for more support for graduate and research assistants. While receiving cordial and sympathetic replies, they have found little success in raising their stipends. There is some resentment among the graduate student council over what they perceive is a financial aid policy in the state that is directed almost entirely to undergraduate students. Because the state legislature initiated the merit scholarship program in 2004, the graduate students have been unhappy that it is only for undergraduates.

THE ISSUE FOR THIS CASE STUDY

Blanchert State University and its home state suffered from an academic "inferiority complex" for many years, as no college or university within the state was held in very high regard, especially by those from outside the Southwest. The academically talented sons and daughters of affluent parents mainly attended out-of-state institutions, although many of them returned to Blanchert State for professional school, and even more of them returned to their home state to live and work. In the late 1990s, some state legislators became aware of state-sponsored merit scholarships for high-achieving high school students in other states, which were designed to curb the "brain drain" in their states by providing a financial incentive to bright students to attend an in-state university. These legislators were impressed with the success of these programs and were also enamored with how popular they were with voters. As a result, leaders in the state legislature began discussions with their colleagues about a state merit scholarship program.

As soon as the idea of this merit scholarship program was introduced, it attracted a great deal of public attention and debate. Advocates for the program claimed it would stimulate young students to work harder in their high school studies, as the scholarship would be awarded purely on their academic achievement. Others lauded the program, hailing it as a long overdue recognition by the state that something had to be done to reward academic excellence and to invest in the future of the state. Opponents of the proposed merit scholarship argued that it should be based on family financial need and claimed that those qualifying for the scholarship would come mainly from affluent families, almost all of whom would be sending their sons and daughters to college anyway. Finally, opponents of the merit-based scholarship suggested that the state could not afford such an expensive program, that the academic qualifications for it were set too low, and that unfair pressure from parents would be placed on high school teachers to award grades that would enable their students to qualify for the scholarship.

After more than 3 years of debate in the state legislature, a bill was passed in 2003, and the merit scholarship program designed to encourage bright high school seniors to attend an in-state university was passed. The scholarship would be renewable on a yearly basis depending on satisfactory academic performance in college and would amount to $4,500 per year. This amount approximated the level of in-state tuition at the state's five public universities.

During the debate over the proposed merit scholarship program, very little input was sought by state legislative leaders from the five public university presidents in the state or the student financial aid administrators. The legislature relied almost entirely on reports about the successful programs already in place in other states and the enthusiastic support and encouragement they received from the voters. Among the voters in the state, the merit scholarship program was popular, and many of them praised their legislators for moving ahead with the program. When the program came up for its final vote in the legislature, few representatives and senators voted against it, knowing how popular it was with their constituents.

The program was put in place, and after only 4 years, the great majority of entering freshmen at Blanchert State University were recipients of this merit scholarship. By the year 2010, more than 85 percent of Blanchert State undergraduates received the scholarship. By almost any measure, the program was a success, and a greater percentage of academically talented students in the state were now attending a university in their state. However, most of the scholarship recipients chose to attend Blanchert State; of the four other public universities in the state, no more than 30 percent of the students qualified for the scholarship. A study conducted on the recipients of the merit scholarship indicated that most of them came from well-educated, relatively affluent families, and that only 7 percent of them were minorities.

Although the program continued to be popular with voters (many of whose sons and daughters were recipients of the scholarship!), in 2010 it had become clear that the state could no longer afford the high costs of the program. Moreover, various political and socially conscious groups around the state were questioning the fairness of the program, claiming it discriminated against poor people and minorities, and that Blanchert State benefited from the program all out of proportion to the other four state institutions.

It was this volatile situation that Blanchert State's new president, Roberta Snyder, faced when she was appointed to her position. She had never lived in the state before assuming her new duties, but nevertheless she was familiar with the state's educational, political, and social history. She had followed the merit scholarship issue closely and was well informed about similar programs in other states. She is determined to enhance the academic reputation of Blanchert State, but at the same time she is an experienced educator with a strong social conscience and for many years has been outspoken in favor of equal opportunity. She has also been an advocate of state and federal legislation designed to remove financial barriers for young people who want to attend college.

She knows that in her first months as Blanchert State's new president, she will be asked what her views about this merit scholarship program are and what she thinks should be done with it, given the dire financial issues faced by the state. She also knows this program has been beneficial to Blanchert State, as it has resulted in a significant increase in the number of academically talented undergraduates enrolling at her institution.

As she contemplates this complex set of issues, here are some options she may consider.

SOME OPTIONS FOR ADDRESSING THIS ISSUE

1. Publicly support the program but make it partially need-based.

President Snyder knows the merit-based program benefits her institution in significant ways. She does not want to lose the outstanding students who are now attracted to Blanchert State. In this option, she testifies to a committee of the state legislature that the state can continue the program and save money by only awarding the full amount of the scholarship to the students from families who demonstrate a substantial financial need. The maximum amount a student from an affluent family could receive would be reduced from $4,500 to

$2,500 per year. This compromise proposal on her part would save the state money and also result in a more equitable use of the dollars. She would also raise the academic qualifications needed for the scholarship, which would result in fewer overall recipients. She believes that the prestige value of the scholarship will continue to provide a positive incentive for students to achieve and to attend her institution.

President Snyder is well aware that this proposal will face vigorous objections from parents of Blanchert State students and from parents of prospective students. By suggesting that the academic standards should be raised to qualify for the scholarship, she also knows she will likely alienate her presidential colleagues at the other four public universities in the state, as fewer of their students will meet a higher standard for the scholarship. She knows the program is popular and that members of the legislature are fearful of public backlash should they eliminate it. With her proposal, she thinks she may have provided them with a face-saving alternative, enabling the program to survive while significantly reducing its costs to the state.

2. Argue for the elimination of the program and create a need-based program.

President Snyder is an educational leader with strong beliefs and values, and she views the state-sponsored, merit-based scholarship program as an ill-advised use of taxpayer dollars. In good conscience, she cannot publicly advocate for this program, even though she is well aware of how much her own university is benefiting from it. She feels that taxpayer dollars should be allocated for students on the basis of need and that it is unethical for the state to use taxpayer dollars to provide scholarships to students whose families can afford to send them to college. She knows that the overwhelming majority of the scholarship recipients in this program would attend college without the program and that academic achievement should be its own reward and should not depend on a financial incentive. In this option, she argues that the money should be used to create a state scholarship program based on need. The current merit-based program would be fazed out when the current students graduate and the need-based program instituted in its place. The state could save money with the new need-based program by allocating less money for it.

President Snyder has to be quite persuasive with her own board of trustees to publicly advocate this position. They likely will feel that the academic quality of the freshmen class at Blanchert State will suffer if her proposal is accepted by the state legislature. She will have to assure the board that this will not be the case. She will face strenuous opposition from parents and voters who believe this program should not be eliminated, especially from affluent parents whose talented sons and daughters would receive no scholarship at all! Some voters may become so incensed with her proposal that they may call on the board of trustees to remove her as president. She is an experienced academic leader, and she was well aware of this before she decided to move ahead publicly with her proposal. She will also face objections from her own campus, in particular from the students. But she feels she would be violating her own educational beliefs and values if she took any other position on the merit scholarship program issue, and she is willing to accept the consequences in her role as president. She believes that this option is best for Blanchert State University in the long run.

3. Urge the state legislature to appoint a blue ribbon task force to study the merit scholarship program and recommend new legislation to resolve the issue.

President Snyder knows this issue is bigger than just her institution and that it is really a state-wide matter. It requires careful study and public debate, and the many constituent groups who have a stake in it need to be heard. In this option, President Snyder feels her best move would be to advocate for a highly visible, state-wide task force to study and consider the issue. This option would also take much of the focus away from her university, which is the institution that has gained by far the most from the 6-year-old merit scholarship program. She knows she will eventually be asked to appear before the task force to share her views about the scholarship program, but she thinks this can be done in a neutral manner by simply describing the pros and cons of various options without committing herself publicly to one point of view. She does not want to alienate Blanchert State's major supporters, alumni, and parents, especially in her first year as president. She is reasonably confident that the state and national economy will recover fairly soon, and she needs the support of the state legislature for the many academic improvements she has in mind for her institution.

Finally, she understands the pressure legislators are under regarding this pop-ular program, and she feels that a respected, state-wide task force would enable the issue to be considered fairly and rationally in the next several months.

President Snyder, by urging the legislature to appoint the task force, may be accused of delaying needed action during a fiscal crisis in the state. Her proposal may be viewed as a bureaucratic response to an issue that others feel should be resolved quickly by leaders willing to make a tough decision. In this option, she may take some of the atten-tion off herself as Blanchert State's new president, but as the president of by far the most visible and influential university in the state, she may not be able to keep her own views private. If the task force rec-ommends a more modest scholarship program that can be funded ade-quately by the legislature, it may receive more state-wide support than one suggested by President Snyder. In this option, she is hoping that a task force may not only take some of the political heat off the legisla-ture for a while, she is also hoping that the task force will develop a positive revision of the scholarship program that will continue to ben-efit her university.

4. Initiate a special fundraising campaign for a need-based scholarship program at Blanchert State.

Roberta Snyder is the new president of Blanchert State, and despite the sag-ging economy, she senses that this situation might present her with an opportu-nity to launch the university's first major fundraising campaign. The Blanchert State Foundation has had some success in the past 10 years, but it has never been challenged to initiate a large campaign. Thus, in the option, President Snyder chooses not to challenge the state's merit scholarship program herself, but to initiate a fundraising campaign at her own institution, a major part of which will be a new need-based scholarship for academically talented students. By taking this action, she is expressing confidence in her own university and its supporters to rise above the current economic recession and work together to improve the university. She knows this merit scholarship issue is highly contro-versial and will be debated for a long time by the legislature. She also feels that using her time and energy to influence the outcome of that debate would be less beneficial to Blanchert State than to initiate a new fundraising effort. Moreover, a need-based scholarship program is more palatable to her and to most of the faculty at the institution. She is reasonably confident that the economic situation will improve and that a 5-year fundraising campaign can be successful. It will demonstrate to the public, the alumni, and the legislature that Blanchert State has achieved real maturity as a major university, and that it has the capacity and determination to improve itself.

In this option, President Snyder is directly challenging her institution to assume responsibility for its own future. She knows there will be skeptics within the university who think she is a dreamer and that her timing for this fundraising initiative is all wrong. She must secure the support of her own board of trustees, of course, before proceeding with this risky venture, and this will require her to be persuasive. She must have faith in her own ability to lead the institution in this direction and confidence in the development staff and alumni of the university. The need-based scholarship idea, as a major component of the fundraising effort, will also have to be sold to the board of trustees, alumni, and friends of the institution. President Snyder knew she would eventually initiate a major fundraising effort at Blanchert State, and she knew it was necessary for the institution to do this to meet its academic goals and compete with its peer universities. She just didn't think she would have to initiate such a program so early in her presidency!

QUESTIONS THAT MAY AID IN THE DISCUSSION
OF THIS CASE STUDY

1. The state legislature, in establishing this popular scholarship program, has unwittingly "created a monster" that it cannot afford any longer and is extremely difficult politically to eliminate, or even modify. Should academic leaders and financial aid officers have been more assertive in warning the state legislature about the program when it was first being considered?
2. President Snyder has strong personal views about equity and equal educational opportunity. To what extent, if any, should her views drive her actions regarding this issue?
3. If a fundraising campaign is initiated by President Snyder and is not successful, what are the ramifications for her and her university?

4. Should President Snyder simply choose not to participate in the public debate and discussion of this issue, asserting that it is a matter best left to the state legislature? How can she or her institution benefit from her direct participation in the merit scholarship debate?

Suggested Readings Related to This Case

Bok, Derek. (1982). *Beyond the Ivory Tower: Social Responsibilities of the Modern University.* Cambridge, MA: Harvard University Press.

McLaughlin, Judith Block. (1992). *Leadership Transitions: The New College President.* San Francisco: Jossey Bass.

Rosovsky, Henry. (1990). *The University: An Owner's Manual.* New York: Norton.

Schmidt, Peter. (2000, February 4). States Criticized for Emphasis Upon Merit Scholarships. *The Chronicle of Higher Education.*

ADDRESSING STUDENT ALCOHOL ABUSE AT HENKEL COLLEGE

SUMMARY OF THE CASE

Henkel College is a private, selective liberal arts institution located in a small town in a Midwestern state. Its 2,100 students come from around the country and are attracted to Henkel for its excellent academic reputation, active extracurricular life, and beautiful campus. Henkel's students are serious about their academic studies, but they also consume large amounts of alcohol, especially at weekend parties on the campus. This alcohol abuse has been a serious concern of the administration at Henkel for many years, but efforts to curtail it have met with almost no success. A great deal of public attention has recently focused on Henkel College, as two students were found dead in their residence hall rooms, both victims of alcohol poisoning after a weekend of partying. The governing board has lost its patience with this excessive drinking problem at Henkel and expects the president to put an end to it.

A DESCRIPTION OF HENKEL COLLEGE

Henkel College was founded in 1839 by three Presbyterian ministers who moved from the Northeast to start a college to provide qualified church leaders for the largely undeveloped but growing area. The college struggled for many years to attract students and faculty and actually closed for 8 years after the Civil War. It was revived through the leadership of Joseph Henkel, a Pennsylvania industrialist, whose wife had grown up in the small town where the college was located. He provided sufficient financial support to restart the college and to recruit a new board of trustees, and the grateful governing board named the college in his honor. By broadening the curriculum, hiring a well-prepared faculty, and improving the physical facilities on the campus, the college was able to succeed, although its enrollment never exceeded 250 until after 1900.

For the next 50 years, Henkel College grew slowly, attracting students mainly from within its state. After World War II, the board of trustees severed its formal affiliation with the Presbyterian church and declared the college independent. The college took advantage of the large number of returning veterans after the war and actively recruited them to enroll at Henkel. As the college grew to almost 900 students by 1958, its curriculum expanded to include extensive science offerings, and it was able to attract many outstanding faculty. During the 1960s and 1970s, when college enrollments everywhere were expanding, Henkel continued to grow, until the board of trustees decided to fix enrollment at about 2,000 students, which it continues to believe is the ideal size for the college to meet its goals.

During the early 1980s, Henkel began receiving a significant increase in applications for its freshman class, most likely due to its solid academic reputation and its excellent success in the numbers of its graduates accepted at prestigious medical and law schools, as well as at well-known graduate programs in business and the sciences. The college regularly received national attention during these years for its high academic rankings in a national magazine. From 1990 to 2010, the college enjoyed unprecedented success, and it was able to attract outstanding students from almost every state and several foreign countries. It was also able to attract and retain excellent faculty who were strongly committed to teaching in a high-quality undergraduate college. Due to the outstanding leadership of three presidents over a period of about 40 years and a supportive governing board, Henkel was successful in building a large endowment. However, since the serious recession of 2008, this endowment has decreased by more than 20 percent in its value, a matter of serious concern to the board of trustees and the entire college.

Henkel College offers academic majors in many subjects but prides itself on the interdisciplinary emphasis in its curriculum. All Henkel students select courses from four basic areas during their 4 years: natural sciences, humanities, social sciences, and mathematics. Courses in these basic areas comprise about one third of students' course work, and all Henkel students are required to pass a comprehensive examination during their final semester. Almost half of the students spend a semester studying abroad, and many of them also write a senior thesis on an issue related to their academic major. Almost 70 percent of Henkel College graduates continue their education after leaving the institution.

The college is located in a town of 9,500 in a rural area of the state. It is a peaceful and attractive community, largely dependent on Henkel College for its livelihood. The town is proud of "its college," although relationships between some of the residents and the college have been strained in recent years due primarily to loud student parties late at night, which frequently have disturbed the townspeople and have sometimes resulted in assaults and property damage.

The president of Henkel College is Matthew Cannon, a biologist who has served in this position for 7 years, after having served previously as the academic dean of a well-known private liberal arts college on the West coast. President Canton is active in raising private funds and is actively involved in national associations that represent the interests of private colleges, especially with the U.S. Congress. He is respected by students, faculty, and staff but is viewed as rather distant and impersonal in his relationships with them.

The dean of students at Henkel is Martha Bright, who has been in her position for 10 years, having come to Henkel from another small college in the Midwest. She oversees a staff of 25 and is responsible for admissions, student health and counseling, career planning, housing, financial aid, recreational sports, and student conduct. At this small college, she is well-known to most students and enjoys cordial relationships with them.

THE STUDENTS AND THE FACULTY

The students now enrolled at Henkel are, by any measure, the most outstanding in its history. Almost 90 percent of the entering freshmen scored in the top 10 percent of the national SAT score distribution, and in high school they excelled in their academic work and leadership activities. Competition for admission to Henkel is rigorous, with almost seven applications for every open space in the entering class.

Most students come from fairly affluent backgrounds, although almost 40 percent of the students receive some form of financial aid, most of it in loans. Henkel has not been as successful as it would like in achieving ethnic diversity at the institution, and in 2010, only about 8 percent of the student body are minorities. The college's rural, Midwestern location and high costs are usually cited as reasons for not being able to attract more minorities. Students from almost every state come to Henkel, and the college actively seeks a national student body. In recent years, about 25 students in each entering class have come from another country.

Student life at Henkel is quite traditional, reflecting its residential, small, liberal arts status. Students are engaged in a variety of social, academic, recreational, service, religious, and political groups, and almost 90 percent of the students live in campus residences and fraternity and sorority houses. The eight fraternity houses at Henkel have been the center of most social activities and parties on weekends for many years. The most popular place for students on the campus is the Henkel College recreation center, which combines exercise and sports facilities with dining services and a student union. The facility was built 10 years ago, the gift of a prominent alumnus of the college.

Students enjoy their time at Henkel, and more than 88 percent of the students graduate in 4 years. Reflecting the aspirations and expectations of their families, about 60 percent of the students go on to graduate schools, as well as medical and law schools. Indeed, Henkel has a reputation within the region as a college whose main purpose is to prepare students for medical and law school, a notion the faculty and administration clearly do not like. Many Henkel students study in another country for a semester, usually during their third year, and this is encouraged by the faculty. Henkel students are not happy with their reputation as "smart, spoiled, rich kids" (as described by students at surrounding institutions!), and perhaps in reaction, they have been active in recent years in service groups in the area and around the state, focusing their efforts mainly on poor and disadvantaged communities.

Henkel College participates in intercollegiate sports at the division III level, and many of its students are members of the college teams in the seven sports for men and the seven sports for women. There is lively competition with similar colleges in their Midwestern-based conference. No students at Henkel receive athletic scholarships, and most of the coaches are part time, as they are also on the Henkel staff or faculty. The sports program provides a good diversion for many students, and most students and faculty are enthusiastic supporters of the college teams.

Since Henkel became much more selective in its admissions in the 1980s, the institution has been able to attract and retain a cadre of outstanding faculty. Previous to this time, most Henkel faculty had received their graduate degrees from institutions within the state or region and were rarely prominent scholars within their academic fields, nationally. However, since Henkel's academic reputation has soared, and with its excellent financial resources, the college has been successful in attracting a first-rate faculty. The faculty at Henkel now come from around the nation and from some of the most prestigious graduate schools. Henkel College administrators have been careful to select outstanding scholars who are strongly committed to teaching undergraduates in a small college setting, and they have been successful at doing this.

The faculty at Henkel College are outstanding. The president and the governing board understand this, and, as a result, compensation for faculty is good and enables the college to compete on a national level for faculty talent. However, with the decrease in the college's endowment since 2008, the president and the board are worried about the college's ability to continue to meet all the financial needs at the institution.

At such a small, residential college located in a small, rural town, the faculty know the students well and are engaged with them in activities beyond the traditional classroom and laboratory. Faculty serve as advisers to student groups, as mentors, as co-members with students on recreational sports teams, and as friends. When recent graduates were asked about what they considered Henkel's best asset, the most frequently mentioned response was "the very strong faculty."

THE ISSUE FOR THIS CASE STUDY

Henkel College is well known in its region as a place where excellent students study hard and drink hard. Its students are highly competitive academically, and most aspire to attend professional and graduate schools. In this competitive environment, stress is a serious problem, and the counseling center staff and the general faculty are keenly aware of the problems students create for themselves as a result of their own high expectations and those of their parents. Resources in the student health center have been increased in recent years in response to these student issues, and the faculty and student affairs staff have tried to make the student experience at Henkel less stressful.

Student social life for decades at Henkel has largely consisted of drinking parties in the eight large fraternity houses and at two bars located close to the campus. Despite the fact that most Henkel College students are under the legal drinking age of 21, purchasing beer and liquor is quite easy, according to students. Either 21-year-old students buy it, students have fake ID cards, or local establishments simply do not pay much attention to the law. Students typically study hard and late at night from Sunday to Thursday. Then the Henkel tradition is that partying starts after dinner on Thursday and continues throughout the weekend. Partying always means alcohol at Henkel, and "getting trashed" is a well-known and generally accepted ritual for some students, who purposely consume large amounts of beer or liquor on weekends to "escape" from what they describe as the "grind." The student affairs staff understands this problem but has been frustrated and perplexed over the years in terms of stopping it. Henkel College is located in a small, almost isolated town, and simply outlawing alcohol anywhere on the campus will only result in students "moving the same problem" to the town itself.

The administration, faculty, and staff at Henkel have tried to address this problem over the past two decades. They have developed good education programs at new student orientation, engaged student leaders in residence halls to talk with freshmen, enhanced support services in the health and counseling center, subscribed to national alcohol education programs, involved the Henkel College parents' council in prevention and support efforts, taken disciplinary action against individual student violators, and placed various fraternity houses on social probation. But the excessive drinking continues. The student affairs staff has been very apprehensive about it, fearing that too many students are putting themselves in jeopardy.

The entire Henkel College community was shocked in the fall of 2009 when, on one weekend, two of its students were found dead in their residence hall rooms, both the victims of alcoholic poisoning.

Both of these students had been at parties, although not together. They were virtually carried back to their residence hall rooms by friends, who deposited them in their beds in their rooms, assuming that they would "sleep it off." The next morning, both of them had died. One was an 18-year-old freshman boy, the other was a 19-year-old girl, a sophomore.

Henkel College responded to these deaths in the most humane ways it could—by working closely with the families and friends of the deceased, by holding memorial services, by providing opportunities to mourn, by inviting students to seek counseling and support, and by trying to avoid placing blame on anyone for the tragedies. Those in the college community somehow struggled to make it through the rest of the semester, and then the college adjourned for the Christmas break in December. Most of the criticism of the college at this time was muted and mild. However, the president, governing board, and faculty knew that they and the college would face bitterness, anger, and lawsuits very soon.

Within a week of the student deaths, the Henkel board of trustees called a special meeting and privately expressed its frustration and anger at President Cannon. The board and president had discussed this problem in previous years, and both knew that their efforts to correct it had failed. The president expressed his deep regret, but the board had lost its patience with this issue and informed the president that his future as president of Henkel College would depend on his ability to "do something positive about this problem now, before another tragedy occurs." President Cannon, already grieved over the death of the students, now was almost overcome with the anger of his board toward him. In the next few days, he considered resigning as president but then decided his love for Henkel College and his dedication to it for the last 7 years obligated him to do whatever he can to address the problems. He also felt he owed it to the memory of the deceased students.

Given the clear expectation of the board of trustees to President Cannon, what options might he consider in addressing this problem? Here are four to consider.

SOME OPTIONS FOR ADDRESSING THIS ISSUE

1. President Cannon, after informing his board of trustees and after consulting briefly with the faculty senate, the student affairs staff, selected student leaders, and the alumni council, should announce that he will use endowment funds from the college to purchase the eight fraternity houses, tear them down, and build new student residence halls in their place, to be staffed and administered by the college. In the process, the president will also announce that fraternities will be banned from the Henkel campus forever. By taking this bold action, the president is sending a clear message to the Henkel College community that he is in charge, that he knows where the problem is, and that he is going to eliminate it.

This option, of course, represents direct and drastic action. It does not include a democratic or collegiate consideration of the issue, which the president has chosen to avoid, because he has little or no confidence that the real problem (the fraternities!) will be addressed. Many of the current members of the board of trustees are Henkel graduates and members of fraternities, as are most of its most prominent male graduates. Student reaction, of course, is likely to be strongly in opposition. Others opposed to the president's announcement may suggest that his action will not eliminate the drinking problem; it will simply relocate it elsewhere. This option requires the president to be willing to be vigorously criticized and challenged and for the board of trustees to stand behind its president. The president is fully aware in this option that his future at Henkel depends on the fate of his decision.

2. President Cannon, confident in his role as leader of Henkel College after 7 years in the position, knows that the college needs a "healing time" of several months before it should take any drastic actions. Despite the board of trustees' anger and admonition to him, President Cannon understands the culture of Henkel College and knows the best solution to this "very tragic incident" is to stay calm and explore additional ways to curb alcohol abuse at the institution. He believes his board's anger will fade, and it will support him. Thus, in this option, he directs the dean of students, Martha Bright, and the

*provost to co-chair a college-wide task force to review Henkel
College's alcohol policies and to submit recommendations to him in 3
months that will "result in a safer and healthier environment" for
students at the college.*

By biding his time via this option, President Cannon is hoping that
the Henkel community will come to the realization that some significant changes in student life must be made. He has not directed the task
force to take any specific actions, but by putting the dean of students
and the provost in charge of the task force, his views and expectations
can easily become known during its discussions. In this option, the
president is honoring the collegiate governing traditions of Henkel
College but at the same time using the task force to enable him soon
to make more serious changes. This option may be viewed as a threat
to students, and if faculty are not strongly represented on the task
force, they may view it as a not very well-disguised effort by the
administration to take unilateral action. Others may criticize the president for delaying action on the problem with a response that is overly bureaucratic, will take too long, and may not result in any changes.

*3. President Cannon is good at analyzing problems, and is convinced
that education is the best solution to this alcohol abuse issue. He is
wary of those who tell him that the way to "handle" this problem is to
make tougher rules, eliminate student groups, and expel students who
violate the alcohol laws and campus rules. He would like for Henkel
College to work to become a "model campus" in providing a healthy,
active, and supportive community to its students and faculty. Thus, in
this option, President Cannon will invite medical, psychological, law
enforcement, and public health experts to the campus to serve as ongo-
ing consultants to the college and to recommend a comprehensive,
health-based plan specifically designed to curb alcohol abuse, reduce
stress, and remove whatever obstacles may be causing the problems.
This process may take a few months, but President Cannon believes it
has the best chance of success, is likely to get the support of the Henkel
College community, and is consistent with his faith in education.*

In this option, President Cannon is hoping that outside experts can
somehow develop a new plan that goes well beyond what the Henkel

faculty and staff have been able to do in the past several years of trying. He is hoping that a coordinated program of education, prevention, and support will result in positive changes. He knows the deaths of the two students have been devastating to everyone at the college, to its alumni, and to the reputation of the institution. He is convinced that this option is the most humane way for Henkel to respond to the tragedy and has the best chance of succeeding. Finally, he believes it is the response that may best restore confidence in Hinkel College. Of course, some of the existing staff and faculty at Henkel may be upset that the president is not relying on them and their expertise but is calling on outside experts to come up with a new plan. The Henkel College community may not be welcoming to "experts" from outside the college who they feel cannot really understand its culture as well as they do. Others may feel this option is just "more of the same"—there is no secret solution to the problem of alcohol abuse on campus; whatever these experts suggest, it will most likely be no different from what has been tried before.

4. President Cannon, in this option, decides that the problem can and must be solved by the student affairs staff, which should start enforcing the rules more strictly, hire and place new staff in each of the eight fraternity houses to supervise activities there, and take tough disciplinary action against student violators. This action would send a clear message to the students that violations of the alcohol laws and campus rules will not be tolerated any longer, and when they are, students will face harsh penalties.

This option, of course, is highly likely to elicit negative reactions from students. It is essentially an action that attempts to "solve" the problem by getting tough with the rules and threatening students with their future at Henkel on being caught as violators. Those who have been disgusted with Henkel's alleged unwillingness to deal seriously with alcohol abusers for years most likely will welcome this approach. Those who are skeptical about this approach suggest that it will simply drive students to drink alcohol elsewhere, thus making the real problem even worse. Becoming enforcers of the rules is not an attractive way of working with students and gaining their confidence, according to the student affairs staff. Henkel College has traditionally had a trusting and caring relationship between its students and its staff and faculty; those who oppose this new "get tough" policy believe it would destroy this important tradition. Advocates for this option argue that in no other community are the citizens able to openly violate the alcohol laws so blatantly. Why should Henkel College students be treated any differently?

SOME QUESTIONS THAT MAY AID IN THE DISCUSSION OF THIS ISSUE

1. The tragic deaths of two students, especially in a small and cohesive college such as Henkel, have a devastating and lasting impact on the institution. When the deaths appear to be ones that could or should have been prevented by the college, it is inevitable in such a tragedy that the president, the faculty, and the student affairs staff somehow hold themselves responsible. This may cause some of them to make decisions that are based more on emotion than reason. Is this evident in any of the suggested options? If so, how can this be avoided?

2. Should President Cannon, when confronted with an angry board of trustees, offer his resignation to the board? If he does not, how quickly should he respond to their demands for action? How can President Cannon understand the board sufficiently well that he knows when to challenge them and when to acquiesce to their directions?

3. What role should the dean of students, Martha Bright, have in dealing with this tragedy and with the overall alcohol abuse issue at Henkel College? She has been in her position for several years and is responsible for student life at the institution. Yet during these years, the alcohol abuse problem has only worsened despite the efforts she and her staff have made to address it. Should the president consider replacing her with a new dean?

4. Right or wrong, institutions sometimes have used times of crisis or terrible events to justify taking actions they have been delaying for some years or that they have not had sufficient courage to put into effect. Does Henkel College already know what needs to be done to curb alcohol abuse on its campus?

Suggested Readings Related to This Case

American College Health Association. (2010). *Healthy Campus, 2010. Making It Happen*. Washington, DC: Author.

National Institute on Alcohol Abuse and Alcoholism. (2004). *National Task Force Report of College Drinking*. Washington, DC: Author.

Presidents Leadership Group of the Higher Education Center for Alcohol and Drug Abuse and Violence Prevention. (1998). *Be Vocal, Be Visible, Be Visionary: Recommendations for College and University Presidents on Alcohol and other Drug Prevention*. Washington, DC: U.S. Department of Education.

Saltz, Robert F., & DeJong, William. (2002). *Reducing Alcohol Problems on Campus: A Guide to Planning and Evaluation*. Bethesda, MD: National Institutes of Health.

Wolfe, Tom. (2004). *Who Is Charlotte Simmons?* New York: HarperCollins.

EVALUATING THE PERFORMANCE OF THE DEAN OF STUDENTS AT CABRERA COLLEGE

SUMMARY OF THE CASE

Everett Mumford has been the dean of students at Cabrera College for 14 years. This undergraduate, private liberal arts college enrolls 2,800 students, and is located in the Southeast. Mumford has responsibility for residence halls, student conduct, counseling and student health, career planning, recreational sports, the student union, and intercollegiate athletics. He reports to the provost, who is the senior internal administrator at Cabrera. Mumford is sometimes referred to as the "Mr. Chips" of the campus and is well attuned to the personal problems and concerns of the students. He is informal and depends on close and friendly relationships in dealing with issues in student affairs. Dean Mumford, who is 48, came to Cabrera from another private college in the Midwest, where he had held various student affairs positions for 10 years. He is under a good deal of stress, related to his job and his personal life, and this has affected his health and his performance as the dean of students. He reports to the provost, who is concerned about his shortcomings as an administrator and about the stress that she is convinced is affecting his ability to lead the student affairs division of the college. The provost knows her campus well and is aware that others share her concerns about Dean Mumford.

A DESCRIPTION OF CABRERA COLLEGE

Cabrera College was founded in 1894 by a group of citizens in the Southeast who wanted to provide a New England-style liberal arts education to young people in the region. The college was provided with generous financial support from Franklin Cabrera, a successful entrepreneur from the East who moved to the area to retire. His substantial gifts convinced the board of trustees to name the college in his honor. His family later continued its financial support of the college, as did some of the major corporations in the state and region.

Cabrera offers academic programs only for undergraduates and has added more technical, science, and business courses to its curriculum in recent years, as its enrollment has decreased by 200 students and interest in traditional liberal arts programs has waned.

Cabrera College is governed by its board of trustees, a group of 16 business, professional, and civic leaders, most of whom live in the region. Its president, Robert Royster, has been at the institution since 2003, and the provost, Margaret Karlsen, has been at the college since 2007. Both came from other private colleges and were attracted to Cabrera because of its fine academic reputation, its tradition of freedom of expression, its substantial endowment ($750 million in 2010), and the opportunity to work with the college's lively and creative faculty and students.

Cabrera is viewed as a unique and somewhat socially exclusive private liberal arts college in the Southeast. Its academic programs in biology, psychology, and English are noteworthy, and many of its students have gone on to successful careers in business, the arts, and the professions. The college is also well known in its region as an institution that attracts creative and individualistic students. During the 1960s, the college was a center of student political activity and was frequently criticized in the press for the sometimes raucous student demonstrations against the Vietnam war and in support of the civil rights movement. Since that time, the college has continued to attract attention for the activities of its students, which are mostly characterized by humorous and artistic expressions about a variety of issues.

Since the recession of 2008, the college has been concerned about its ability to attract the number and academic quality of students it needs. Applications have decreased, and the relatively high cost of attendance ($44,000) is believed to be a major reason for this decrease. The endowment has lost about 20 percent of its value in the past 2 years, and President Royster is spending more and more of his time away from the campus trying to raise money for the college.

THE STUDENTS AND THE FACULTY

The students at Cabrera mostly come from the Southeast, although in previous years the college was able to attract more students from the Northeast and the Midwest. The great majority of them are from affluent families, and all of them are enrolled on a full-time basis at the college. Cabrera is reasonably competitive in admissions, with more than two thirds of the entering students having been in the top 25 percent of their high school classes.

Students are mainly attracted to Cabrera College for its sound academic programs, its pleasant campus, and its well-known reputation for creativity. The tolerant, open culture on the campus is appealing to many young people who are nonconformist in their lifestyles or who have been rebellious in some aspect of their lives. There are many zany traditions in student life, and in dress, physical appearance, and actions, the students frequently seem to be trying to outdo one another to attract attention. Most of this is done with good humor, and there is easy acceptance for those who are "unusual!"

Students seem to love their experiences at Cabrera and revel in the freedoms they have to express their individuality. The level of academic stress is not high, but because so many of the students are seeking to find themselves and to explore various lifestyles, their use of counseling and health services is high. Alcohol and drug abuse are serious problems that the college has been dealing with for many years. Students at Cabrera cherish their reputation for zaniness and view student life at larger, state universities as boring, conforming, and obsessed with athletics.

Almost all of the students at Cabrera are white. The college has made efforts to recruit more minorities, but its high costs, rural location, and reputation as a place for nonconforming students have prevented it from achieving success in diversifying the student body. Almost one third of the students participate in a travel-abroad experience during their years at the college. However, among Cabrera's 3,300 students, only 25 come from other countries.

There are about 75 student organizations at the college, but this number varies from year to year, as the students love to create their own, new groups and seem to compete with each other for the most outrageous and humorous names. While many of their activities are frivolous and purposely crazy, the students are active in community service, especially with disadvantaged children and school programs. For several years, Cabrera students have conducted their own "arts in the schools" program, teaching dancing, singing, and painting with young children.

Reflecting the informal and imaginative nature of student life at Cabrera, the student government seems to change from one year to another depending on campus issues and especially on the whims of the students at the time. The students usually reject any suggestion of a hierarchical decision-making model and seem to prefer the open and often chaotic "town hall" method of conducting their business. Student groups at Cabrera often express their views to college officials on various issues, but it is difficult to determine who is speaking for the student body, if anyone! Moreover, students traditionally love to spoof their elders at Cabrera and to dream of ways to confuse and befuddle the administration. These antics are an accepted way of life at the college and contribute to the lively and often unpredictable nature of life at Cabrera!

The faculty at Cabrera have been attracted to the college because of its commitment to teaching, its pleasant atmosphere, and its welcoming culture. Most faculty teach three or four courses per semester, advise students, and know their students well. Most of the faculty share the values of openness, freedom of expression, and individuality with their students. The faculty seem to love the college, and few of them leave it once they begin their teaching at Cabrera.

The gap between faculty and administrators often seen at other colleges and universities is not obvious at Cabrera. At this small college, most of the faculty are involved in working with college leaders in various projects, curriculum discussions, the hiring process, and student life. The faculty maintain close relationships with students, and many of them participate with students in a variety of social, recreational, and arts-related activities. Some of the faculty even join with student groups in their zany and creative activities, and others are the humorous targets of various pranks conducted by students. Everyone seems to enjoy this activity.

Faculty governance at Cabrera can best be described as fluid. Over the years, there have been attempts to form a faculty senate, with actual by-laws and committees, but these efforts have never resulted in much success because most faculty strongly prefer a spontaneous and

bureaucracy-free approach, rallying supporters to support some particular issue at the time. This has made it challenging for the provost,
Margaret Karlsen, to know how to gage "faculty views" on various
matters. However, because he knows virtually all of the faculty by
name and works with them closely, she is able to rely on her good
relationships with the faculty in making decisions.

The faculty may reject formal organizations they think may stifle
their activities, but they are actively involved with the curriculum at
Cabrera. They take their teaching seriously and are strongly committed to the values of a liberal arts education. When a new course it suggested to be added, it results in lively debate and scrutiny, as does any
proposal to change the academic requirements for a particular major.
Some of the faculty are engaged in research, although this is not a
major activity of the faculty at Cabrera. They feel attached to the college and its future and pay close attention to how the college is func-
tioning.

THE ISSUE TO BE ADDRESSED IN THIS CASE STUDY

Dean Everett Mumford is known to almost everyone at Cabrera
College and is viewed as an amiable, avuncular, and honest man by
students and faculty. He loves his work and feels comfortable at this
college, whose students might otherwise drive other student affairs
deans to distraction given their often zany antics and creative activities. Moreover, he is also good at establishing rapport and trust with
students, many of whom are experiencing serious personal and developmental issues in their lives. Although formally an administrator, he
spends most of his time with individual students, befriending them and
helping them cope with their often complicated lives.

Mumford has rarely paid adequate attention to his administrative
duties, preferring to spend his time helping students with their personal problems and issues. This was the reason his responsibility for
the admissions and financial aid offices at Cabrera was removed in
2005. The provost at that time felt Mumford had not given strong
leadership to these two offices and was concerned with the decreasing
number of applicants to the college and with the number of complaints from students and their parents about financial aid. The admissions and financial aid offices now report directly to the provost.

Dean Mumford was disappointed when he lost the responsibility for these offices but rationalized it to himself by saying it would give him more opportunity to deal directly with students. He loves the college and its students and is on campus about 60 hours per week. He knows he worries too much about his job and rarely exercises or takes vacations. He continues to be on campus long hours, and he never refuses to meet with a student who wants to see him. He is now 48, and after being married for 18 years, his wife divorced him in 2007. This change in his personal life was difficult for him, and he responded by spending even more time on campus and by drinking too much alcohol. He has managed to meet most of his obligations on campus, but instead of the alcohol relieving his stress, it began to affect his work at Cabrera. For the most part, however, he was able to hide his increasing dependence on alcohol from his colleagues and students on the campus.

By 2009, Provost Margaret Karlsen knew that there were financial problems with the residence halls at Cabrera, that the college union facility badly needed renovation, and that the poor communication between the athletic director and the recreation program director was causing serious problems for students in both programs. All of these areas at the college are under the direction of Dean Mumford.

Provost Karlsen has real affection for Everett Mumford, and appreciates his hard work and his ability to work with the challenging students at Cabrera. She also admires his caring and sensitive response at the college last year when a student took her own life in a campus residence hall. But she is concerned with the administrative problems in the student affairs division and Mumford's apparent inability to resolve them. In her conversations with Dean Mumford about these matters, it becomes clear to her that he is under a good deal of stress, and after a while, he admits to her that he is drinking too much.

As Provost Karlsen thinks about this situation, she knows she must do something to resolve it. The following are some options she is considering.

SOME OPTIONS FOR ADDRESSING THIS CASE STUDY

1. Convince Dean Mumford to take a 6-month, paid leave of absence, require him to participate in an alcohol abuse recovery program, and regain his health.

Provost Karlsen believes Everett Mumford is under considerable stress and wants him to regain his health. She is convinced that if he does not do something about his health problems now, his condition will only get worse, and his job performance will continue to deteriorate. In her conversations with Mumford, he insists that he is fine, can handle his problems, and does not need any medical assistance. He tries to assure Karlsen that he will cut back on his drinking and redouble his efforts to correct the administrative problems within the student affairs division. The provost is patient with him but firmly denies his requests to continue in the dean's role for now, and she informs him that his only choice is to accept the paid leave of absence. Mumford eventually agrees to this arrangement but is worried about who will do his job while he is gone and how his absence will be explained to his staff and students at the college. The provost assures him that she will handle this and that no mention will be made to anyone about his alcohol problem. She writes a letter of understanding for Mumford to sign, indicating that, on successful completion of his alcohol rehabilitation program and her assessment of his health after the 6-month leave, he will be reinstated in his position as dean of students.

In this option, the provost is giving Mumford a chance to rehabilitate himself, retain his dignity, and return to his position. This action requires her to be firm and decisive and to explain his absence to the college community. It also requires her to make arrangements for someone else to assume his duties for the next 6 months. She knows that, because of his warm personality and friendly relationships with students, his absence will be obvious. She decides to ask an associate provost in her own office to assume Mumford's position on an acting basis for the next 6 months. She will meet in person with the student affairs staff at the college, inform them of her decision, and ask for their understanding and support. During this 6-month period, she knows she cannot put off attending to the various administrative problems in the student affairs division and will expect her acting dean to address them as best he can. She plans to meet periodically with Mumford during his leave of absence and provide him with encouragement as he faces his problems. She is reasonably optimistic that this approach will result in Mumford's successful and healthy return to his dean's position, but she also knows that it will be a difficult challenge for Mumford. She feels he has made many positive contributions to Cabrera College during the past 14 years, and she wants to see him return and be successful.

2. Hire a team of outside consultants to evaluate the effectiveness of the student affairs division at Cabrera College.

The provost knows there are communication problems in student affairs among some of the department heads, that there is a deficit in the housing operation, and that the union building has been neglected. She is also aware that her predecessor moved the admissions and financial aid offices out of the student affairs division some years ago because he had lost confidence in Everett Mumford's ability to provide strong leadership to these critical functions. However, she still believes that Mumford is a valuable and hard-working dean who is well suited to work with Cabrera's unique and challenging students. In this option, she decides to invite a team of three experienced senior student affairs officers from similar private colleges to come to the campus and evaluate Cabrera's student affairs organization. She hopes that their insights and suggestions may result in substantial improvements and new ways of addressing student issues and administrative problems. She knows this action on her part will likely make the current student affairs staff quite uncomfortable and defensive, but she assures them that their jobs are not in jeopardy and that her goal is to improve the overall effectiveness of the division. The provost is not naïve and is aware that some of the student affairs staff are concerned about the lack of good leadership from Dean Mumford and may question the provost's motives in her use of outside consultants. But she decides to proceed with this plan and is reasonably confident that she will receive a report that will improve the effectiveness of the student affairs division.

By inviting an outside team of consultants to Cabrera, the provost is sending a clear signal to Mumford and the student affairs division that some important changes need to be made. She is purposely vague about these changes because she is confident that the consultants will be able to indentify the problems and make useful suggestions for improvement. She prefers this approach to one where she would intervene herself and make whatever personnel and organizational changes she feels are needed. She knows this process will be difficult for Dean Mumford, but in her own mind she hopes that it will also result in some improvement in his administrative performance. She is concerned about his stress and the associated health problems he is facing, and she intends to stay in close touch with him as he copes with his situation. She knows that this external evaluation process will contribute to his stress, and she suggests to him that he seek some counseling. She hopes the consultants will help the student affairs division improve but is not overly optimistic about this. She believes the major problem in the division is the lack of strong leadership by Mumford. While the consultants were not asked specifically to evaluate Mumford's performance, she expects them in private conversations with her to confirm her belief. If things do not improve in the student affairs division, the report may serve as a basis for further action she may take.

3. Reorganize the student affairs division and restructure Mumford's position.

The provost, who is the senior academic and administrative officer at Cabrera College, knows there are problems in the student affairs division and feels it is her responsibility to resolve them. The staff has good relationships with students but does not communicate well with one another, has ignored some financial and maintenance problems, and lacks strong leadership. She has lost her patience with the ability of Dean Mumford to turn the student affairs division around, but she is not willing to terminate him because she feels he has made positive contributions to students and can continue to do so. In this option, she informs Mumford that he will retain his title but will report to an associate provost in her office who will assume administrative responsibility for student affairs. The directors of the various student affairs departments will report to the associate provost. Mumford will retain his title as dean of students but in fact will function as a general "counselor to students" at Cabrera, a role he has assumed for years. He will be relieved of his administrative responsibilities for the student affairs division. Provost Karlsen knows this new arrangement will come as a shock to Mumford, and she hopes it will not result in his resignation. In conversations with him, she urges him to accept this new assignment and tells him that she hopes it will relieve some of the stress he has been under. She is frank in her discussions with him about his drinking and urges him to seek counseling. She is reasonably confident that this new administrative arrangement will result in substantial improvements in the student affairs division, as the associate provost who will become the administrator of the division is a strong and decisive leader.

By selecting this option, Provost Karlsen has decided she needs to do something to solve the problems in the student affairs division and, at the same time, make it possible for Everett Mumford to continue to be a contributing member of the Cabrera College community. She knows this is an unusual arrangement and that she will certainly have to revisit it in the next 2 or 3 years. She will have to convince Mumford that he can accept this new role and retain his dignity and self-respect on the campus. But she is concerned about his health and does not think he can provide the needed leadership for the student affairs division. She is stopping short of removing him altogether from the college and is trying to provide him with an opportunity to do what he does best—befriend and support students. She knows that no other person at Cabrera is as able as Mumford in working with the creative and challenging students at the institution. She does not want to lose this asset, and she believes that, in this new role, Mumford can continue to be of value to the college. Finally, she is hopeful that by relieving him of his administrative duties, she might lessen the stress he has and that he might return to good health.

4. Terminate Mumford as Dean of Students and hire a new leader for the student affairs division at Cabrera College.

The provost has worked with Everett Mumford for the last 5 years. Although she likes him and respects his dedication to students, she has lost confidence in his ability to lead the student affairs division. She has shared her concerns about the division with him several times and has not seen any improvements. She feels the various problems in the division are the result of his lack of leadership, and she is convinced that he will not be able to provide better leadership in the future. She is concerned about the stress in his personal and professional life, and she has made genuine efforts to help him deal with it, including his recent drinking problem. Thus, in this option, Provost Karlsen decides to relieve Mumford of his dean of students position and begin a search process at once to recruit and hire a new dean. She will give Mumford a year's leave with pay, after which time he will no longer be employed by the college. She regrets having to take this action but feels she gave Mumford more than enough time to improve his performance and that this is the best thing for the college. She knows that he is a popular man on the campus and that there will be objections to her action, especially from students. But she feels it is her responsibility to do what is best for the college and is willing to deal with the criticism that will come with this decision. After she informs Mumford of this decision, she meets with the student affairs staff, explains what she has done, asks for their support, and describes what their involvement will be in hiring a new dean.

This option is frustrating and painful for Provost Karlsen because it represents to her a failure to correct the problems in the student affairs division. She feels she made a good faith effort to improve the division and Mumford's leadership, but she was not successful in doing so. While she recognizes that the termination of a dean is something she is expected to do if the circumstances warrant it, she does not enjoy the process. However, she knows that she probably delayed this action for too long, hoping that her admonitions to Dean Mumford would result in positive change. Her previous experience as an academic leader has convinced her that strong, new leadership can often resolve lingering problems and result in positive improvements. Now that she has taken the action to terminate the dean, she feels some relief and wonders why it took her so long to do so! She will continue to offer her assistance and friendship to Everett Mumford, hopeful that he can regain his health and move on to another academic position within the next year. Finally, she must now move on with her effort to recruit and hire an outstanding leader as the new dean of students at Cabrera.

QUESTIONS THAT MAY AID IN THE DISCUSSION OF THIS CASE STUDY

1. To what extent, if any, should provost Karlsen involve her president in this situation?
2. Everett Mumford was popular with and well known to students. How should the provost respond to the objections of these students to a change in the dean's role?

3. Alcohol abuse is a common and serious problem that affects faculty, staff, and administrators. Should the provost have recognized this problem earlier and done more about it?

4. Assuming (Option 4) that Everett Mumford regains his health and interviews for another student affairs position elsewhere, what should provost Karlsen's response be to an inquiry about his suitability for such a position?

Suggested Readings Related to This Case

Barr, Margaret, & Sandeen, Arthur. (2007). *Critical Issues for Student Affairs: Challenges and Opportunities.* San Francisco: Jossey Bass.

McCaffery, Peter. (2010). *The Higher Education Manager's Handbook: Effective Leadership and Management in Universities and Colleges.* New York: Routledge Publications of Taylor and Francis.

McClellan, George S., & Stringer, Jeremy. (2009). *The Handbook of Student Affairs Administration.* San Francisco: Jossey Bass.

Tierney, William G. (1999). *The Responsive University: Restructuring for High Performance.* Thousand Oaks, CA: Sage Publications.

RESTRUCTURING CAREER SERVICES AT CLAIRE STATE UNIVERSITY

SUMMARY OF THE CASE

Claire State University, a comprehensive, land-grant institution located in the Midwest, enrolls 42,000 students. It has extensive graduate and professional school programs and has established a solid academic reputation. The university is quite selective, and its graduates are sought by employers from around the country. In 2010, the board of trustees named a new president, and in view of the serious budgetary problems in the state and at Claire State University, he has notified each of the vice presidents that their budgets will be reduced in the next year by 10 percent. The vice president for student affairs is responsible for the career services office and must decide how to reduce its budget while continuing its operation.

A DESCRIPTION OF CLAIRE STATE UNIVERSITY

Claire State University was founded in 1884 as a public, land-grant institution and has enjoyed good financial support from the state for many years. It grew rapidly after World War II, and now, in 2010, is one of the outstanding public research universities in the nation. Its professional schools of law, medicine, veterinary medicine, and dentistry, together with its 10 colleges and large research programs, make Claire State a truly comprehensive university. The institution also has a highly visible and popular intercollegiate athletics program and active, loyal alumni. Due to the wise leadership of several previous presidents, the Claire State University Foundation now has an endowment of more than $3.5 billion. The great recession of 2008 has result-

214

ed in a 30 percent reduction in the endowment, a matter of serious concern to the new president and board of trustees.

Claire State's board of trustees, appointed by the governor of the state, was pleased to attract John Buddford as its new president in 2010. He had been the provost at another large and well-known land-grant university in another state for the past 5 years. As an economist, Buddford was also well known as an expert on university finance, and the board of trustees was attracted to him partly for this reason as well as his excellent record as an academic leader.

The professional schools at Claire State are almost autonomous, although the deans of the four schools report to the provost. The 10 colleges are agriculture, engineering, arts and sciences, journalism, business administration, education, architecture, fine arts, health education, and biological sciences. The arts and sciences college enrolls the most undergraduates, and the colleges of agriculture and engineering have the highest number of graduate students. The faculty are strongly committed to research and, during the past calendar year, attracted more than $400 million in external funds to conduct their research. Despite the recession, the faculty at Claire State continue to be successful in securing support for their research, which is a matter of considerable pride at the institution. Most of the funds to support this research go to the school of medicine and the colleges of engineering, agriculture, and biological sciences.

Claire State is located in a city of 40,000 and enjoys mostly positive relations with the community, which is known as the main "college town" in the state. When alumni and others inundate the campus and city for fall football games, it is transformed into a large and happy rally for the institution. This enthusiastic support for Claire State's athletic programs has contributed significantly to its popularity and to the pride its graduates have for their alma mater.

The vice president for student affairs at Claire State is Margene Cook, who has been in the position since 2005. She previously served as the senior student affairs officer at another public university on the West Coast. She has responsibility for admissions, housing, financial aid, career services, student life, recreational sports, counseling, student health, and the student union. In her 5 years at Claire State, she has earned a reputation as a caring and thoughtful administrator who understands students and is strongly committed to helping them achieve their goals.

THE STUDENTS AND THE FACULTY

The undergraduate students at Claire State come primarily from within the state. Competition for admission is especially strong for the 20 percent of the undergraduates who come from other states. The university is popular in its state and region, and in 2010, there were almost five applicants for each place in the freshman class. The students mostly come from middle- and upper income families and are attracted to Claire State because of its strong academic programs and the successful records of many of its graduates over the years. While almost 20 percent of the students go on to graduate and professional school, most of them enter the workforce on completing their undergraduate degrees.

The most popular fields of study in 2010 for Claire State undergraduates are business administration, engineering, accounting, biology, and economics. In the past 10 years, programs in history, psychology, education, journalism, and fine arts have experienced declining enrollments of undergraduates.

Reflecting the relatively homogenous population of its state, Claire State University's minority enrollment is only about 10 percent. Almost half of these students come from other states, the result of fairly aggressive recruiting programs begun in the late 1980s. The entering freshman class at Claire State in 2010 had the best academic qualifications in the institution's history, with more than 80 percent of the students ranking in the top 15 percent of their high school classes. The relatively low cost of attending the university, together with its good academic reputation and positive campus life, are usually mentioned as the primary reasons for the increasing interest of such outstanding students in the applicant pool. Only 25 years ago, Claire State was accessible to all state high school graduates who were in the top half of their classes.

Students like attending Claire State and are active in social, religious, recreational, and community service organizations. Almost 40 percent of the undergraduates live on the campus in residence halls or Greek houses. Interest in sports is high, and there is little political activity on campus. Most Claire State undergraduates complete their studies there, are proud of their degrees, and expect to move on to jobs in business, engineering, and other areas.

Undergraduate students at Claire State University regularly used the various student services on campus and take them for granted. Most of them are unaware that part of their tuition each semester is earmarked for support of such services as the student health center, the student union, and recreational sports. Tuition is in the middle range for public, land-grant universities, and about half of the students receive some financial aid, mostly in loans.

The graduate and professional school students at Claire State come from around the nation and from other countries as well. They are a much more diverse group than the undergraduates, and, of course, most of them primarily focus on their work in specific academic departments. There are 4,200 international students at Claire State, and almost 80 percent of them are in graduate programs, especially in agriculture, engineering, and the biological sciences.

Graduate students are primarily attracted to Claire State because of its academic reputation, comparatively low cost, availability of teaching and research assistantships, and the opportunity to study with a specific professor in their field of study. Competition for admission to the professional schools is rigorous, and, as a result, since about 1980, most students admitted to these programs are residents of the state, a reflection of intense pressure from the state legislature to support its own citizens.

The focus of some graduate programs in the last 10 years has been more strongly on professional preparation and jobs. While most PhD graduates still move into academic, governmental, and research positions, increasing numbers of master's degree program graduates view their degrees as the best means of getting a job, especially in business administration and engineering. Claire State has provided extensive assistance to its students in their job searches and placement for many years, and this is increasingly the case with graduates of its master's degree programs.

The faculty at Claire State University are relatively young, as a large group of them, who had been hired in the academic boom era of the 1960s, have recently retired. As a result, these newer faculty are much more diverse and, at the same time, more research oriented.

Claire State understands that its academic future is dependent on the quality of its faculty, and, as a result, the recruitment of top faculty has been the number one priority at the institution for at least the last 20 years. By almost any measure, the university has been successful in this regard. Faculty salaries and professional development opportunities are among the best at public, land-grant universities, and most faculty seem to enjoy their work at Claire State, and most of them stay.

The faculty have been quite successful at attracting external funds for their research, doubling the institution's research funds in just the last 10 years. They have been encouraged and supported in their efforts by their departments and colleges, by the provost, and especially by the institution's office of research. Despite the recession of 2008, the faculty have continued to achieve success in the competitive world of winning research grants. The new president of Claire State, John Buddford, is delighted with this hard work by his faculty and plans to emphasize it to state legislators to demonstrate to them what the university is doing to advance the economic, social, and scientific goals of the state.

The faculty at Claire State are not much interested in institution-wide administrative or financial issues, except when there are matters that directly affect them. They are active in their own departmental and college issues, especially those having to do with the curriculum. Since the recession of 2008, there has been increased activity in the almost dormant Claire State faculty senate because of concern about the cutbacks in various academic and support programs at the university. The faculty senate is anxious about what the new president may do with the budget.

THE ISSUE FOR THIS CASE STUDY

Claire State University has a new president and is facing a serious financial situation due to decreased support from the state legislature. The college and department will be required to develop budgets with 10 percent fewer dollars than they had the previous year. This has resulted in a great deal of discussion and much anxiety among administrators, faculty, and staff. Moreover, with the economy still not in recovery, the state legislature has announced that a tuition increase cannot be implemented because of public opposition to any such measure.

The career services office is a centralized facility designed to serve students' career planning, exploration, and placement interests. It is a state-funded program within the division of student affairs at Claire State, and its director reports to the vice president for student affairs. The career services office is located in the large student services center on the campus and is used heavily by students. Despite the economic recession, Claire State's graduates are sufficiently sought after by employers. Many corporate, governmental, military, and nonprofit organizations continue to visit the career services office to interview and hire its students. The 20-member staff of the office have worked closely with these employers over the years and have cordial relationships with them.

In the past 15 years, the career services office has expanded its efforts to serve students, especially in the area of career counseling. The staff has been aware of the difficulty that many undergraduate students have in deciding on a career and in making realistic and informed decisions about their future. Thus, the career services office hired additional counselors during this period and worked closely with faculty in the colleges at Claire State in helping students clarify their career goals. The office also made significant advances in computer-assisted services during these years, enabling student and employers to access useful career and personal information, which often saved time and money for those who use the office. The career services office is now considered a leader in its field in the computerization of its programs for student and employers.

This popular service for students and employers at Claire State has been in operation for almost 65 years and is often mentioned during campus tours and in new student orientation as one of the finest assets of the university. Free of charge to students and employers, the office represents a fine example of cooperation between the university and the corporate sector, a partnership that benefits both. Students, faculty, staff, and employers appreciate the work of the career services office and take it for granted.

Now, in 2010, the career services office is faced with the need to make significant financial cutbacks in its operation. Margene Cook, the vice president for student affairs, has to decrease her overall budget by 10 percent and is considering several options for the career services office. She is disheartened by this situation, as the recession has made it much more difficult for students to get jobs; at the same time, she has to decrease the services designed to help these students in their career exploration and decisions. The following represent some of the options she is considering.

SOME OPTIONS FOR ADDRESSING THIS ISSUE

1. Vice President Cook has worked hard to establish trust with the deans of each of the colleges at Claire State in the 5 years she has been on the campus. She stays in regular touch with the deans, making sure the various departments for which she is responsible are well known to them and getting feedback from them about how her division of student affairs can serve their needs. She is respected not only by the academic deans at Claire State but also by the provost for her diligence in addressing problems and her positive relations with students. She knows that it is important to Claire State University to continue the cooperative relationship between the institution and the corporate sector via the career services office. It is the place where students "go to get jobs," to use the students' vernacular. She does not want to lose the current services, but she knows her budget cannot continue as it has. In this option, Vice President Cook decides to approach the college deans and present them with a proposal. Her plan is to decentralize the career services office by moving some of its services (and salaries!) to the colleges themselves. She would transfer five of her current career services to the colleges, and she would continue to pay half of their salaries. The other half would be paid by the colleges out of external funds they generate from various corporate grants. By doing this, she argues to the colleges that they and their students will benefit from a more personal, college-based staff member directly responsible to their college. By doing this, she will not only decrease her own budget but will retain the essential career services for the students. By sharing these five staff members with the colleges, she is retaining their jobs, decreasing her own budget, and enhancing cooperation with the colleges in helping students obtain jobs. She knows this proposal represents an additional expense for the colleges at a time when they face the same requirements to cut back that she does, but she knows this is a small amount for them and that their students will benefit.

By taking this action, Vice President Cook is relying on the trust and good relations she has built over the past 5 years with the college deans. She must convince them that this small investment on their part (out of nonstate funds!) will not only serve their students well but will enhance their relationships with employers. In this action, she must also convince the career services office director and staff that this is not a "breaking up" of the office structure but, in fact, a wise move to collaborate directly with the colleges. This is an option, she believes, that will enable her to continue the essential career services to students, assure employers that Claire State will continue to work closely with them, and satisfy her own serious budget requirements. She knows she will have to be persuasive with the college deans to get their support for this proposal!

2. Vice President Cook believes in the beneficial partnership between the university and the corporate sector in serving students' needs. She is especially committed to the basic fairness of the arrangement and to the equal access all students have to interviews and possible employment. Moreover, she is proud that students and employers do not have to pay a fee for these services. The career services office is funded entirely from the Claire State budget, and Cook believes this approach has been well received by students and employers. However, in this option, Cook decides that with the current budget crisis, Claire State simply can no longer afford this luxury. Thus, she proposes to impose a new "career services fee" of $10 per semester for all students, the fee becoming part of their regular tuition. This modest fee can be imposed by the board of trustees without having to secure legislative approval and will be earmarked for support of the career services office. At the same time, she will require a user fee by employers to gain access to the career service programs and the university's students. This annual fee will be scaled to the size of the company or organization, but all employers will have to pay the minimum user fee of $2,000 per year. No employer would be granted any kind of privileged status in this arrangement; all would have equal access to Claire State students. By selecting this option, Vice President Cook is proving that she can continue to operate this essential office without using funds from the regular university budget, yet can retain the integrity of the office and its services to students. Moreover, this option would enable her to retain all of the current staff.

Vice President Cook is counting on her ability to convince her new president that the imposition of this "career services fee" for all students is a good idea, even in such difficult financial times as 2010. She is also relying on her ability, and that of her staff, to convince others that this small, required fee will be accepted by the students. Although the student government association at Claire State does not have veto power over any proposed fee increases, the common practice is that the student government association will be consulted regarding it. Asking for a fee from employers, she knows, will require some good faith conversations with them, hoping and anticipating that their long-time support for Claire State will cause them to continue using the career services office. Of course, she knows that Claire State's graduates are the most sought after in the state, and thus the employers most likely will be willing to pay the fee to retain access to them. Cook also writes an agreement to be signed by employers and the university, assuring that this new fee arrangement will retain the integrity of the student–employer relationship and the full and open access of all students to prospective employers. She has some concern that some students and employers may choose to bypass the career services office entirely and conduct their own job searches, with no direct contact with the institution.

3. Vice President Cook is keenly aware of the increased use of computer-based, private job search and placement organizations throughout the country, and especially in such a tight job market as exists in 2010, she knows that these firms would like to have access to Claire State's graduates. She has carefully studied what these private firms claim to do for applicants, and she knows that they would fall far short of what the Claire State career services office can offer, especially in the areas of career planning, self-assessment, and career exploration. While the career services office at Claire State has become quite sophisticated in its own computer-assisted services to students, she believes she can move even further in this direction and, in the process, save enough money to meet the requirements of the 10 percent required cutback. Her plan, which will be quite painful for her to implement, will consist of laying off four full-time staff and replacing the services they provided via a new computer-generated system of helping students with their career planning and exploration. She strongly dislikes having to terminate full-time staff, but in this budget crisis, she see few other options. By taking this action, she is demon-

strating her ability to make difficult decisions in order to retain an important set of services, albeit in modified form. Despite her dismay over having to let four full-time staff go, she prefers doing this on her own to having someone external to the career services office or to her student affairs division handle the budget cutback.

By choosing this option, Vice President Cook is trying to deal realistically with the budget problem while also moving the career services office even further into the computer age. Although she suspects that new technologies developed in the near future may result in significant changes in traditional campus-based career services offices, she remains convinced that there is an important place for personal, one-on-one counseling about careers, and this is something colleges and universities can do best, especially when there is no profit motive involved. Thus, in this option, she is moving Claire State's career services office closer to a stand-alone, computer-based operation than before, and she worries about whether the students and employers will accept and be satisfied by this approach. She will see opportunities for the four laid-off employees, especially within her student affairs division, in such offices as housing and student health, both of which operate as auxiliaries, being supported entirely by student rents and fees.

4. Despite the critical nature of the current budget crisis, Vice President Cook does not want to rush into any decision without giving it careful thought and especially without involving others openly in considering various options. She is known as a fair person and as an administrator who will listen to her staff and others before making a decision on important matters facing the student affairs division. She respects the staff in the career services office and feels they have done a fine job of meeting student and employer needs over the years. Thus, in this option, Cook decides to appoint a task force composed of three members of the career services office, three faculty from Claire State colleges, three employer representatives, and three students to "study the issue and recommend to her a solution which will retain the high quality career services and also, meet the budget cutback requirement." She places the task force on a short timeline and informs them to submit their report to her in the next 4 weeks. She has asked the retired Dean of Students at Claire State to chair the task force. By choosing this option, Vice President Cook is placing her faith in the collegial model of seeking a solution to this problem. She knows this will be difficult for the task force, and she realizes that some critics may view this action on her part as just delaying what must be done. Finally, she hopes to retain some of the trust she has built among her staff, the colleges, the employers, and her own students at Claire State by involving them in the process.

Vice President Cook is not only "buying some time" with this option, she is also hoping that the task force will present her with a way of solving the budget problem that she can accept and that will be supported by her staff and the colleges. She knows this involves a risk on her part, as the task force may recommend something that will be unacceptable, whether to her or to her president. This is a difficult challenge for the task force, and she has some previous experience in seeing such groups not having the courage to recommend decisions that will negatively impact current programs and staff. If the task force gives her something she cannot accept, she must make a decision on her own regarding the career services office. But she knows if the task force does its job well, the staff, students, faculty, and employers who were responsible will feel they have made a positive contribution to a difficult problem and will no doubt be supportive of the career services office in the future. In appointing the members of the task force, Vice President Cook had to be careful not to appoint well-known "friends" of the career services office. For its report to be credible, she knows the task force must include staff, faculty, students, and employers who are open to many options and must have the freedom to make whatever recommendations it feels are best for Claire State University.

QUESTIONS THAT MAY AID IN THE DISCUSSION
OF THIS CASE

1. Vice President Cook has had less than 3 months to work with the newly appointed president of Claire State. How should she try to assess the new president's priorities, decision-making style, and patience in this process? Should she simply proceed on her own in the manner she has been used to for the past 5 years or should she check with him in advance about the options she is considering?

2. What arguments might Vice President Cook use in Option 1 to convince the college deans that it is in their best interest to pay part of the salaries for her staff? Are there other alternatives with the colleges if the deans reject her proposal?
3. Is it fair or ethical for Vice President Cook to try to solve this budget problem by imposing a new mandatory fee on the students? What should she do if the student government association, speaking on behalf of the students, recommends against any such fee? Should this fee also be imposed on graduate and professional school students, who make comparatively little use of the career services office?
4. What obligation, if any, does any college or university have to the future employment of its graduates? Is this a service that could be provided just as effectively by a private company, external to the institution? Is it no longer feasible for higher education institutions to provide such services, especially without cost to either students or employers?

Suggested Readings

Bok, Derek. (2003). *Universities in the Marketplace: The Commercialization of Higher Education.* Princeton, NJ: Princeton University Press.

Bolles, Richard N. (2009). *What Color Is Your Parachute, 2010? A Practical Guide for Job Hunters and Career Changers.* Berkeley, CA: Ten Speed Press.

McClellan, George S., & Stringer, Jeremy. (2009). *The Handbook of Student Affairs Administration.* San Francisco: Jossey Bass.

Reardon, Robert C., Lenz, Janet G., Sampson, James P., & Patterson, Gary W. (2008). *Career Development and Planning: A Comprehensive Approach.* Belmont, CA: Brooks/Cole.

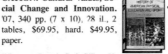